BUT YOU'RE STILL SO YOUNG

BUT YOU'RE STILL SO YOUNG

*How Thirtysomethings Are
Redefining Adulthood*

KAYLEEN SCHAEFER

DUTTON

DUTTON

An imprint of Penguin Random House LLC
penguinrandomhouse.com

LIBRARY OF CONGRESS CATALOGING-IN-PUBLICATION DATA
Names: Schaefer, Kayleen, author.
Title: But you're still so young: how thirtysomethings are redefining
adulthood / Kayleen Schaefer.
Description: New York: Dutton, an imprint of Penguin Random House LLC,
[2021] | Includes bibliographical references.
Identifiers: LCCN 2020039795 (print) | LCCN 2020039796 (ebook) |
ISBN 9781524744830 (hardcover) | ISBN 9781524744847 (ebook)
Subjects: LCSH: Adulthood. | Self-realization. | Life cycle,
Human—Psychological aspects. | Conduct of life.
Classification: LCC HQ799.95 .S32 2021 (print) | LCC HQ799.95 (ebook) |
DDC 305.242—dc23
LC record available at https://lccn.loc.gov/2020039795
LC ebook record available at https://lccn.loc.gov/2020039796

Printed in the United States of America
1   3   5   7   9   10   8   6   4   2

BOOK DESIGN BY KRISTIN DEL ROSARIO

Some names and identifying characteristics have been changed to
protect the privacy of the individuals involved.

For Julien

CONTENTS

BUT
YOU'RE
STILL SO
YOUNG

INTRODUCTION

You turn thirty, and you do the inventory.
You go over the arbitrary list that we impose
upon ourselves and panic about not completing.

—MARCUS

It was the end of the workday for Marcus, who's thirty-six and lives in Austin. He's an auditor for the state of Texas. He was supposed to meet his parents, who had come to town from Houston to attend a pecan festival the next day. He was going to pick them up at their hotel; they were heading to dinner from there.

He'd had a bad day at work, just another one of many recently. He'd been in meeting after meeting where he and his team had been berated about projects they were supposedly screwing up. If his parents hadn't been there, "I would have drank and gone to bed," he says.

Marcus is lighthearted and makes jokes often. He's the kind of person who always sounds like he's smiling when he's talking, even if he isn't, so it's jarring to hear him be so despondent. He's been looking for new jobs, increasingly desperately. His eye has started to twitch, his sleep is inconsistent, and, at work, he's gone from thinking *I don't want to work here anymore* to knowing *I can't work here anymore.*

In the mornings, he often wakes up in a good mood, then lies in bed for an hour.

I could go to work, he thinks.

Then he thinks, *Why?*

"I physically feel myself getting sick at the idea," he says. "I can feel it kicking in."

He thought he was close to getting a new job. He got to the second round of interviews for an auditor position with the city of San Antonio, which is about an hour and a half from Austin. He was poised—and excited—to move, even with the $10,000 pay cut, but found out a few days before his parents' visit that he didn't get it.

When he got to their hotel room, he was reeling about not getting the job and, in general, feeling like he had no control over his own life.

Six years ago, on his thirtieth birthday, he'd panicked about his life not looking anything like he imagined it would after college.

He made a mental list.

Job? *Check.*

Wife? *No.*

House? *No.*

Kids? *No.*

He started worrying about what he didn't have and comparing

himself to other people, who he assumed had the spouse, two-story house, and small dog he thought he'd find for himself. He fretted: *Was his life enough?*

I thought my life would follow a certain order too. I would check off one thing before moving on to the next. The broad outline went like this: complete school, establish a career, save money, get married, have children. I didn't think I had to do all these things before I turned thirty, but I assumed I'd do them *in* my thirties. The promise of this timeline comforted me. It offered me order within what often felt like a frenetic, rootless existence in which I spent half my nights watching reruns of *30 Rock* on my computer in bed and the other half going out until well after midnight. Even if the friends I hung out with all the time weren't following that linear path, I assumed most of my peers did, at least according to what I saw on my social media scroll and what I heard from my mom about acquaintances back home.

When I turned thirty, I was still languishing, with almost nothing checked off my life list. I had barely established a career, and yet, still, I felt like any minute I'd be rushing through these milestones, hurling toward a place where I could stop, where I'd feel like I'd arrived.

———

But you're still so young.

Anyone in the struggle of trying to figure out why certain parts of your life aren't anchored the way you thought they'd be has heard this, usually from a well-meaning older person trying to convince you your life is not as big a mess as you're sure it is (no one younger than you would say this). Sometimes you might even hear it in your own head as a pep talk, when you're looking in the mirror, wondering who the reflection in front of you is going to become, or while you're lying in bed, finding it hard to get up.

But you're still so young.

You have time.

Keep going.

In the 1950s, sociologists identified five milestones that, when completed, mean a person has fully transitioned into adulthood. Much like what I had instinctively defined for myself, they are (1) completing school, (2) leaving home, (3) becoming financially independent, (4) marrying, and (5) having a child. In general, in the 1950s and for decades afterward, these milestones were completed by the early thirties at the latest. They were often achieved even sooner, in the late teens or early twenties. In 1975, US Census data shows that 45 percent of women and men had attained the traditional markers of adulthood by the time they reached thirty-four.

But today, cultural shifts and economic turmoil have changed both whether these milestones feel necessary and if they are attainable. "Many [young people] have not become fully adult yet—traditionally defined as completing school, landing a job with benefits, marrying, and parenting—because they are not ready, or perhaps not permitted, to do so," sociologist and University of Pennsylvania professor Frank F. Furstenberg Jr. wrote in a 2004 report examining what it means to become an adult in America today, research funded by the MacArthur Foundation. In 2016, according to census data, just 24 percent of women and men had completed these milestones by the time they reached thirty-four.

We start working only after finishing the advanced degrees we're told we need to compete in an information-based economy (and, in many cases, accumulate substantial debt while doing so). We have less financial stability than young people before us, due to many factors, including school debt, the modern gig economy, stagnant wages, and repeated economic upheaval, caused by the 2008 financial crisis and, most recently, the coronavirus pandemic. We return to our parents' homes after we thought we left for good, either because we can't afford our own places or because we're not sure yet where our dreams will take us. We marry at our own pace, if at all. And, if we decide we want children, we try to have them when we feel ready, a delay driven by women's wider range of career options as well as assisted reproductive science that can make childbearing possible past our most fertile years.

"The timetable of the 1950s is no longer applicable," Furstenberg wrote.

———

But you're still so young.

It's true that we do have time, and we're taking it. Tom W. Smith, who, for four decades, directed the General Social Survey, a large sociological data-gathering project run by the National Opinion Research Center (NORC) at the University of Chicago, thinks the age of completing school, getting married, and having kids is only going up. "I do think it has to hit a plateau, but I don't think it has hit that yet," he says. "In another ten or twenty years, we're not going to be talking about this as a delay. We'll be accepting this as the normal trajectory."

But what's implicit in anyone telling you "But you're still so young" is the idea that eventually you'll get to some sort of standardized adulthood. We're told to follow these kinds of timelines, that if we do we will be happy with our lives. Shaking them up, either by rejecting certain milestones, or accepting that we may not be able to achieve them, goes against what we're taught. These markers are supposed to be some sort of an end. When we arrive at them, we will know what we're doing and who we are. "The life events that make up the transition to adulthood are accompanied by a sense of commitment, purpose, and identity," Furstenberg wrote.

Which is why right now it feels to me like we're caught in the middle. On one side we're tethered to the history of how the thirties have been lived in the past—there's this assumption that we want to replicate that—and on the other, we're establishing our own adult landmarks, like moving across the country, switching careers, or freezing our eggs. We're taking time to figure out what we want, dealing with misfortunes we can't control, and realizing our lives might not look the way we thought they would.

I started reporting this book before the COVID-19 pandemic and continued during it. As I write this, there is no certainty about what the widespread health, economic, political, and social repercussions of the pandemic will be. The immediate reality of the virus, and the death, sickness, and economic destruction it's causing, is devastating, and months in, it still feels like life is mostly on hold—a freeze that has only added to the difficulty of trying to structure our thirties how we want them to be. In the best cases, the upheaval of the pandemic has been freeing and clarifying, a pause where we could figure out if what we did day-to-day made us happy—what we missed as well as what we didn't, told us about ourselves. But no matter what, any changes we might want to make, whether we were fantasizing about new careers, new relationships, or new homes, seem harder than ever to execute—and some momentum stopped completely. Many thirty-somethings found themselves grieving the loss of a loved one, unable to pay their rent, being furloughed indefinitely from their job, or postponing marriage in part because they can't have a wedding. It also centered the fear that may have been on the edges of our consciousness before: we may never get where we want to be. Our thirties could already feel staggeringly impossible to figure out, but now, in the midst of all this instability, believing you can achieve what you want can seem delusional. It's harder than ever to see our dreams and go after them.

It's also easier than ever to feel alone right now, even if logically you understand that you're not the only thirtysomething whose plan has to be reimagined. Even before the pandemic, I wanted to share my story and the stories of other people who are still figuring out the decade, but especially now, it seems essential to talk about our lives, with their magical moments and their heartbreaking ones—and by doing this, mesh together some kind of comfort that we're working our way through adulthood as authentically as we can.

————

When I turned thirty, I was living with two roommates in an apartment on the sixth floor of a walk-up building. The kitchen, dining area, and living room were all in a single space. We shared one bathroom. Our furniture was secondhand, which meant we had a love seat instead of a full-size couch and a heavy wood dining table that was too big to place in the middle of the room. An inflatable moose head hung on the wall.

One of my roommates turned thirty a few months before I did. He ended his night of reveling by puking in the bathtub. I was appalled, both by the vomit I saw the next morning when I went to shower before work and the statement the scene seemed to make: he wasn't trying to make his thirties any more settled than his twenties.

I would not be doing this. I wanted my celebration to be grown-up. I was turning thirty! I hired a sommelier and invited my friends to my apartment to smush into the kitchen/dining area/living room for a wine tasting. I thought it would be elegant.

It was a shitshow. The sommelier droned on about the wine even though no one wanted to listen, including me. At one point, he stood on a chair to get us to pay attention, but we still didn't. When he finally stopped talking, he started flirting aggressively with my engaged friend in front of her fiancé. Everyone got extremely drunk because the only food I served was what I considered to be fancy appetizers, like bacon-wrapped dates.

From my apartment, we went to a dance club where my two most unsteady friends crashed into a table and broke it. We got kicked out, and I turned thirty on the sidewalk in front of the club.

I'd judged my roommate for what looked like a haphazard approach to his thirties, but despite my best intentions, my thirties were also off to a rocky start. And the road since has been anything but a straight shot.

When I began this book, I was thirty-nine and still not fully transitioned into adulthood, at least not according to the milestones sociologists say I should have hit. Some of what I wanted to accomplish, I have. But other ways of making my life feel established have taken, and *are* taking, so much longer. When I look back on my thirties, they weren't what I expected. What I thought I'd resolve in a few years—marriage, a secure career, children—stayed up in the air for most of the decade, and some of it is still unknown. But the longer I took to figure out what I wanted, the more comfortable I got with the uncertainty. As a result, on my best days, I felt like I was earning my achievements, after struggling with them both inwardly and outwardly. They seemed right and exciting when I got there, not like I was pushed into completing them because of my age.

The thirties have not been studied very deeply. Many sociologists and academics have researched and examined the twenties and have acknowledged that this decade is different than it was before. This time can be, and often is heavily encouraged to be, about finding yourself, about experimenting, about playing with different possibilities for your future.

Jeffrey Jensen Arnett, a psychology professor at Clark University in Worcester, Massachusetts, first started studying the twenties in the early 1990s. He was aware of what was happening in the culture. "You could already see how the median age of entering marriage was rising," he says. "More and more people were getting more and more education as the economy was changing more to a knowledge economy. People were waiting later to have their first child."

But he was also in his early thirties and feeling like an adult for the first time. He was teaching human development and family studies at the University of Missouri and began to ask his students and others in their twenties in the community around Columbia, Missouri, "Do you feel you have reached adulthood?"

He talked to more twentysomethings, broadening his sample to include young people in New Orleans and San Francisco. He included working-class as well as wealthy people, those who'd never gone to college and those still in school, people who were supporting themselves and those whose parents were paying their bills. A little more than half his sample was white, 18 percent

African American, 16 percent Asian American, and 14 percent Latino. More than three hundred interviews and survey responses led him to believe we should be thinking about these years differently than we ever have before. Arnett posited that these twentysomethings were in the midst of a period that was a precursor to adulthood, one that had not yet been explored as a life stage. He called it "emerging adulthood."

In an age when "adulting" is a verb that is deployed for achievements as mundane as owning more than one bath towel or buying a houseplant, Arnett's work may not seem revolutionary. But at the time, his idea that there was a gap between appearing like an adult and actually feeling that way, and the concept that those years came with their own psychological makeup, wasn't rooted in popular knowledge. Now, twentysomethings taking years to settle into their identities seems obvious enough to cause eye-rolling, but in 2000, Arnett's article in *American Psychologist* stating that 60 percent of his subjects felt like both grown-ups and not-quite grown-ups was provocative.

At the time, most psychologists agreed with German American developmental psychologist and psychoanalyst Erik Erikson, who theorized that adulthood was divided into three stages: young (roughly ages twenty to forty-five), middle (about ages forty-five to sixty-five), and late (all the rest). But Arnett thought "young adulthood" was too broad a term to apply to a twenty-five-year span that included college students and people in their forties.

"The basic idea is that it's helpful to think about the twenties as a new life stage that's not just an extended adolescence and not just the same thing as the young adulthood that comes after," Arnett says.

Arnett described these emerging adults as self-focused and uncertain about their futures—a lot of them talked about feeling frustration and a sense of not quite understanding the rules of how to go about their lives. But he also heard a lot of positivity. When he asked if they agreed with the statement "I am very sure that someday I will get to where I want to be in life," 96 percent of them said yes.

In "emerging adulthood" we are still seeking—and making decisions about—the lives we want. We are exploring what we desire and what we reject. We are considering, and maybe trying to lock in, where we want to be, what we want to do, and who we want to love.

"The freedom of the age period is something that's really never happened before," Arnett says. "People always went right from their family household to a new household. They married and they had their own family, and now we have this period of a decade or more where you live apart from your parents. You make your own daily decisions. You run your own life. That's a new experiment. And so far, at least from their accounts, it's very successful. They thrive on it."

This isn't to say that the twenties are this way for everyone, or that hundreds of years ago there weren't people in this age group who were "emerging adults," even though Arnett hadn't labeled them yet. Some psychologists disagreed, and still disagree, with Arnett's framing of "emerging adulthood" as a development stage. According to them, it can't be one because unlike during, say, infancy or puberty, everyone in the age group isn't going through the same physical and mental changes at around the same time.

"It's a concept that describes some characteristics for a few young people," says Richard Lerner, a professor of child study and human development at Tufts University in Medford, Massachusetts. "It's certainly not a concept that is reflective of a universal period of development for all young people who are moving from adolescence to the early adulthood years."

It's true that we all proceed on our own timelines and step into different points of our lives at our own pace, either because of our own choices or something external that makes what we want possible (or impedes it). There have always been people bouncing between ambitions and homes and relationships while others the same age have already cemented the major points of their lives. The difference, I think, is that now, whether you use the label "emerging adulthood" or not, more of us than ever before have been through a period of trying out different selves. The country, and parents, are more permissive about letting twentysomethings follow their passions, or even mild interests, in any direction they want without having to create something more permanent. The provision of the Affordable Care Act that allows children to stay on their parents' health insurance until the age of twenty-six is widely liked. And the more economically privileged you are, the more leniency you are likely to have. Experiences like spur-of-the-moment moves to other continents, months spent back in childhood bedrooms, jobs that end in less than a year, or romantic relationships that linger longer than they should don't have to add up to anything.

But then from this period where anything goes we have to enter our thirties, a decade for which no one has given a new label. No one on high has said it should be laid out any differently from how it's always been, which seems impossible, as if we're supposed to snap to wanting all the traditional adult milestones, and be able to set them in place in an instant. There's a supposition that the freedom of our twenties has a finite end and we should solidify our lives simply because one decade has ended and another has started.

———

But you're still so young.

This can also mean the opposite, a sarcastic way of telling yourself that you're not, in fact, *that* young.

One of my favorite scenes from the movie *Wedding Crashers* is when John (Owen Wilson) and Jeremy (Vince Vaughn), who are both in their thirties, are sitting on the steps of the Lincoln Memorial at dawn, passing a bottle of champagne back and forth, after another season of partying and hooking up with bridesmaids at nuptials they weren't invited to.

"You don't think we're being . . . a little irresponsible, I mean . . . ?" John says.

"No, one day you'll look back on all this and laugh and say we were young and stupid, a couple of dumb kids running around," Jeremy says.

"We're not *that* young," John says.

I have a real fear of being behind, even if I swear I don't care what other people do. I think most people do.

As I got closer to forty, I started looking at my life, and all of what I hadn't accomplished in my thirties, and I got scared. I worried I was alone. I had read about people marrying later, people having unstable career paths, people struggling financially, people not buying homes, and women having children after their peak fertile periods had ended, but the statistics weren't much comfort when I was twitching and anxious and certain *I'm doing it wrong.*

I worried that no matter what the numbers said, everyone else had done more in their thirties than I had. They were where they thought they'd be, and I was the one who couldn't get it together. Everyone else had gotten off the bus, while I was still sitting in the back, daydreaming as I looked out the window.

I wanted to know I wasn't alone.

————

When Marcus got to his parents' hotel room, he sat down and stared out the window. It was raining, and he realized he didn't want to go to dinner or anywhere but the chair he was currently in. "Everything came to a head," he says. He was exhausted by not being able to move forward with his life.

His girlfriend, who he calls L, lives in Chicago. They'd been dating long-distance for two years. Now, she wanted to find a job where he was and move to him. The problem was: Marcus didn't know where he was going to be. He was looking for jobs all over the state.

If he'd gotten the job in San Antonio, he could have told her to try to get a job there too, and they could have started planning what life would look like if she did. But he didn't, so on the night with his parents he had nothing he had to do—or wanted to do—besides stare out the hotel window and watch the rain.

His parents tried to cheer him up. They told Marcus he'd figure it out. This was just a blip, they said. The situation was temporary. He just had to wait. Marcus wanted to believe this, but "that's sort of like saying, if someone were stabbing you, and you were like, 'Eventually their arm is going to get tired.' What you'd really want is for them to stop stabbing you immediately."

It wasn't so much that he was frustrated by not having gotten to specific milestones, like getting married, or buying a house, or having kids—he still had those in his mind, but as he'd gone from his early thirties to his midthirties, he stopped feeling as much pressure to arrange his life according to that structure. "It becomes less relevant to me the older I get," he says. "It's kind of wild. I've gone half my life without it now. I might as well go the other half. I say that about the house, the kids. It's still on the list, but I'm like, *I've gone thirty-six years without checking these final boxes off.*"

It was more the idea that now, even if he decided he wanted those things, he didn't know how to get them. All he could see was that he didn't have a safe exit out of his job or know what to tell L about where she should move—and that meant that there was no clear way to think about a longer-term future for possibly getting married and having kids.

"Decision ten can't be made until decision one and two are figured out," he says. "It's not that I don't know. I need someone else to tell me. I don't like that. I like to be in control of my own life."

He was thinking he needed to see a therapist, that he had tried to figure this out for himself and was failing, something he told his parents.

They never left for dinner; instead, Marcus spent the next three hours staring at the rain.

———

Like Marcus and me, the seven other women and men in this book envisioned their thirties differently than how they are actually living them. Charles thought he'd be done with his degree (and paying off his debt). Sally thought she'd be married. Yasin thought he'd be wealthy. Nick and Muriel thought they'd be famous comedians, and Adam didn't think he'd be a stay-at-home dad. Abigail thought she'd have a child.

But what they all have in common is: They're not done yet. They're working through how their dreams are morphing and changing, and what their altered realities mean for how they continue through the decade—and the rest of their lives.

Some are at the beginning of their thirties, others are in the middle or closer to the end. They live all over the country, come from various races and backgrounds, and have disparate incomes and debts.

But they are individuals and not intended to represent all thirtysomethings. Rather than take a definitive look at everyone in the decade, I was interested in people who were still filling out their lives, seesawing between the freedom of not knowing what comes next and the terror of not having a map. People who didn't know when, or if, they'd get there, or if they still want what they once thought they did.

The individuals I followed are all part of today's sprawling middle class, and have the mind-set and security that comes with that. They are privileged enough to feel like they have options: they're attempting to arrange their thirties according to their desires. But they aren't so well set up that they're certain they can make the lives they want.

They told me about their victories and their failures, their good moments and their bad. Sometimes they felt close to getting what they wanted; other times they were down and defeated. They shared all of themselves, from the most granular aspects of their days to their big, overarching apprehensions and yearnings about the future.

I organized their stories around the milestones sociologists say make us adults: (1) completing school, (2) leaving home, (3) marrying, (4) becoming financially independent, and (5) having a child. This isn't because I want to sanction these benchmarks, but at some point most of us will grapple with them. They're the framework society has given us. You could be working on your degree. You could be struggling to pay for your own place. You could be contemplating marriage. You could be questioning how to save enough money to feel secure. You could be deciding whether you want kids.

No matter what we're striving for, or what we have to accept we're never going to get, it's all hard. Adulthood no longer has to follow a strict order. Nothing is required, but that also makes everything unknown.

It feels wrong to admit: *I'm still working on it. I don't know if this is right. I thought it would be different. I can't do this.* But this is how so many of us are proceeding through the decade.

We're not going back to a time when adults checked off milestones in lockstep, but that doesn't mean that together we're not changing what the thirties look like. We're redefining the decade through our individual decisions and collective adaptation to an evolving culture and world.

———

It's instinctual to want order, to demand an answer to the question: *How does it end?*

But this story isn't about an ending. It's about a new way of moving through our thirties. We're confronting the goals that have been dictated for adulthood for ages and making difficult decisions about what we want and what we have to let go.

We're structuring our lives in ways that fit our own comfort level and abilities. We're bending them to the outside forces we can't control and also to our individual advantages and disadvantages. We're answering a different question: *Where will that take us?*

We all know how it goes. Some days are a slog, others fat with possibility. We alternate from pushing ourselves to surviving however we can. There are triumphs and setbacks, false starts, retraced steps, and continued effort. The goals and timelines we set for ourselves can be modified or disappear. But no matter what, our lives aren't being poured neatly into adult molds. Instead, we're figuring out our thirties ourselves.

We want so much. We don't know if we'll get it. We're still so young.

CHAPTER ONE

Completing School

———

I remember when I was twenty-two, and someone said,
"Oh, I'm thirty-one," I just thought they were so old,
and now I'm thirty-one, and I don't feel old at all.

—CHARLES

I used to assume that when I grew up, my life would look like an adult's in the 1950s. Back then, in both the middle class and popular culture, it went down like this: A man and a woman married. The man worked. The woman probably didn't. They owned a house in the suburbs, had kids, and ate dinner as a family every night.

I started picturing this as a kid. I'm white and was raised middle-class, and even though I grew up thirty years after the fifties, in the eighties, my parents' lives were playing out like fifties versions.

They married when they were both twenty-six and are still married. They were raising my brother and me in the suburbs of Dallas, where they'd bought a house. My mom had been a teacher, but quit before I was born, and didn't go back to work until I was in middle school. When my dad came home from the job he wore a suit to, she had dinner ready for the family. After we were done eating, my dad would tell my brother and me, "Help your mother," then disappear for the rest of the night.

As I got older, toward the end of high school and in college, I started to have doubts about whether I really wanted this life. As a high school graduation present, my mom and my aunt took me to New York City. I walked around, openmouthed and immediately in love. I thought to myself, *I'm going to live here one day.* After I graduated from college, I moved there to try to become a writer. The immediate future I wanted was to own an apartment and live by myself in the city. Marriage felt like it could wait a long time. I wasn't sure I ever wanted kids. But, still, I kept looking toward the 1950s model of adulthood. I saw the house, the husband, and the kids as my endpoint, no matter what else I fantasized about.

It's confusing to me still. *Why was it the standard I kept looking to? Why couldn't I shake it off even though I was clearly trying to figure out my own version of adulthood?*

Tom W. Smith, the former director of the General Social Survey, says the fifties are so pervasive, in part, because a huge percentage of the current adults, mostly baby boomers, a generation that was born from 1946 to 1964, grew up during that time. They watched their parents live like that, even if they didn't do it themselves. "You can't have a living memory of what America once was in the 1920s because there aren't enough people left," Smith says. "But there's more than enough who grew up in the 1950s to make that part of living memory."

Plus, it was the advent of television, and the images from that time are some of the most iconic of American life. The neat, low-slung houses. The square yards. The picket fences. The mom in an apron. The dad setting down his briefcase. The two kids watching television while lying on their stomachs on the floor.

The collective memory, and the idealized pictures, have resulted in romanticizing the time period—there's a feeling that life was easier then. Some of this perceived ease comes from people having a script to follow. Adults were expected to live a certain way. "Marriage was considered to be universal," says Steven Mintz, a historian at the University of Texas at Austin and the author of *The Prime of Life*, a book about the challenges of modern adulthood. "It wasn't a decision you made. Even many gay people got married [to someone of the opposite sex] because it was assumed they would. The assumption was that marriage was part of the script of life. Buying a home was part of the script of life. Having children after marriage was part of the script of life."

This script made it so that people didn't have to make any choices about how to go about their lives—they knew how their stories would end. So even though that meant that they were constrained to the *Leave It to Beaver* model, they also didn't have to agonize over whether to marry the person they liked at the moment, wait for someone who might be an even better match, or not marry at all. They didn't have to choose between staying in a job or going back to school. There was no question they were having children. "There were certain psychic benefits of this pattern," Mintz says. "My own personal view is that we have far more options now, and that's generally a good thing, but it does produce this incredible sense of pressure, stress, and anxiety."

Stephanie Coontz, a historian and the author of *The Way We Never Were*, which takes a critical look at Americans' nostalgia for the 1950s, doesn't agree that things were better back then either, but she understands longing for a time when all of your choices were made for you. "When people walk into a store with too many choices, they sometimes walk out because they're overwhelmed," she says. "And as we have more choices about our lives, it becomes more difficult, more anxiety-producing, than when it was, *Oh well, there are two choices: vanilla or chocolate.*"

A few months after Yasin's thirty-first birthday, he said to his business partner of the networking app for sports fans they founded, "I can't believe I'm thirty." She told him that he was actually thirty-one. "It did not register to me that I had hit thirty," he says. "Not just hit thirty but was a year and a half into my thirties. It just didn't register."

What mostly registers for him these days is the pings alerting him to new tweets, chats, emails, or texts as he works. His life is marked by a string of beeps. It's easy for him to be in front of his computer and not know if he's been there for one hour or four. "There's so much that's getting done that I can't even pay attention to the time anymore," he says.

In his twenties, he worked in finance at J.P. Morgan and Morgan Stanley, managing money for executives at publicly traded companies, and got promoted at both banks. These jobs made him lots of money, which he'd wanted ever since he was in college at Drew University in Madison, New Jersey, where he majored in economics and political science and minored in Middle Eastern studies.

Yasin is intense and driven, obsessed with making his app a success. He mostly talks about work and uses plenty of corporate-speak, bringing up "benchmarks" he wants to achieve and speculating about when "things should hit for me." But he shares his emotions too, even if that means confessing envy or tears. In college, "I felt like everyone around me had money," he says. "They had more than I did, and I felt insecure about it." Classmates were driving Range Rovers bought for them by their dads, who were managing partners at investment banks. Yasin's parents had emigrated to the United States from Turkey and moved between jobs and business opportunities trying to earn enough to support him and his three siblings. They owned their home in Lincoln Park, New Jersey, where he shared a bedroom with his three brothers, but there were never long stretches when the family knew they'd have plenty of money. Sometimes they were doing well; sometimes they weren't.

At school, Yasin didn't have a car and got free housing because he worked as a resident assistant in his dorm. He took extra shifts at his job waiting tables and spent his tips on a used Mercedes, his first attempt at feeling less inferior to the rich kids around him. *I know I can work harder than these people*, he told himself. *I'm going to hustle and I'm going to get it done.*

For a while his career in banking gave him exactly what he wanted. "I was farting money," he says. But he didn't actually know what to do with this money. He had nothing he wanted to spend it on. Yasin is Muslim and doesn't drink. He didn't want to go to nightclubs until 3:00 a.m. He wanted to get up early and ride bikes with his friends. "I thought I had everything figured out when I was twenty-five," he says. "I had nothing figured out. I had money, and that was it."

———

Beyond the fifties being idealized as a simpler time, they are also thought of fondly because the country was doing well economically. Jobs were plentiful, wages were good, and consumer debt was almost nonexistent.

The majority of America was middle-class. That meant having a household income of between $3,000 and $7,000 a year, according to Mintz (that's between $32,000 and $75,000 in today's dollars).

"The gap was the difference between having a Chevy and having a Buick," he says. "It wasn't like having a BMW." Most people owned houses too. "You could work at a factory and own a cottage by a lake," Mintz says. "You didn't feel like you were poor. You felt like you were doing great."

But the reality of this prosperous era was that it disproportionately benefited white men. White women had access to the middle class primarily through marriage, not through their own achievements, and African Americans were kept out almost completely. Government policies, as well as universities, business owners, and housing developers were set on excluding them from gaining any wealth. "They were the bottom of the heap," Coontz says.

During World War II in 1944, the government passed the GI Bill, which is best known for giving veterans free college tuition. By 1956, some 2.2 million veterans had taken advantage of this, but even though 1.2 million Black men had fought in the war, in segregated ranks, they were effectively excluded from the new law. What was then called the Veterans Association encouraged them to apply for vocational training instead, and in some cases, arbitrarily denied their educational benefits.

If Black veterans did apply to school, Northern universities were slow to let them in, while Southern colleges refused them entirely. "Though Congress granted all soldiers the same benefits theoretically," historian Hilary Herbold writes in *The Journal of Blacks in Higher Education*, "the segregationist principles of almost every institution of higher learning effectively disbarred a huge proportion of Black veterans from earning a college degree."

Not having a degree prevented them from getting more-secure, better-paying jobs. African American men were mainly hired for low-level, manual-labor jobs, both by commercial businesses and government organizations. Even Black college graduates could sometimes only find these kinds of positions. And after they were hired, they couldn't get promoted. In Memphis, for example, big companies International Harvester, Southern Bell Telephone, and the Memphis General Depot employed Black men only at the lowest pay levels.

There was "no greater instrument for widening an already huge racial gap in postwar America than the GI Bill," historian Ira Katznelson writes in his book *When Affirmative Action Was White*, about racial inequality in the twentieth century.

———

As time went on, the civil rights movement helped minorities begin to be accepted into college in greater numbers (more women than ever before were attending too), and the government introduced other bills that would assist with the cost. The National Defense Education Act of 1958 gave financial aid to students studying science and technology who might help the United States gain an advantage over the Soviet Union. The Higher Education Act of 1965 subsidized poor and working-class students.

But the government had also shifted from paying tuition outright to an increasingly complicated system of federal and private loans. At first, this seemed fine. The credit card was becoming popular, and Americans were getting more comfortable with the idea of personal debt. Besides, college was seen as a good investment, a way to guarantee you'd get a high-paying job with benefits. In 1972, President Richard Nixon created Sallie Mae, which was then a government-sponsored student-loan company.

Attendance kept increasing in the 1980s, but so did tuition. From the late 1980s to the present, tuition has risen at a rate of four times that of inflation and eight times that of household income.

The income range for the middle class has ballooned too. Today, households with an annual income of anywhere from $40,000 to $250,000 count themselves in the middle class.

And many of these families can no longer afford to send their kids to college. For students, leaving school with debt has become as common as leaving with a favorite cheap beer. According to estimates, forty-five million people in the United States have school debt, and the total is about $1.5 trillion, which is more than Americans owe on their credit cards or car loans.

Journalist M. H. Miller took on more than $100,000 in debt while earning a BA and MA from New York University, with his father as a cosigner on the loans. While he was growing up, his family had just enough money to pay their bills, and what things cost was a constant topic of conversation. But when it came to the $50,000 a year his education would cost, his parents told him repeatedly, "We'll find a way to pay for it."

After Miller graduated, most of what he thought about was how he was going to make his loan payments. With every paycheck he got, he subtracted the amount he needed for rent, as little food as he could live on (a carton of eggs and a can of beans), and one of his loan payments. His paycheck was never big enough. "How I would eat or pay my rent without defaulting was a constant refrain," he writes in an essay for the *Baffler* about struggling to pay his debt. "At my lowest points, I began fantasizing about dying, not because I was suicidal but because death would have meant relief from having to come up with an answer. My life, I felt, had been assigned a monetary value—I knew what I was worth, and I couldn't afford it, so all the better to cash out early."

One afternoon at a diner in Brooklyn, he asked his father what would happen to the debt if he did kill himself. Matter-of-factly, his dad answered that he would have to pay the debt by himself.

Then his dad smiled, which Miller writes, "I sensed had caused him great strain."

"Listen," he told his son, "it's just debt. No one is dying from this."

Today, Miller is in his early thirties and no longer shares the debt with his dad. Instead, his wife helps him with the monthly payments when she can, "a small, depressing victory, a milestone perhaps unique to members of my generation," Miller writes.

His debt is roughly the same amount as it was when he started repaying it, but it no longer affects him as explicitly as it once did. "After ten years of living with the fallout of my own decisions about my education," he writes, "I have come to think of my debt as like an alcoholic relative from whom I am estranged, but who shows up to ruin happy occasions."

———

Charles, who's thirty-one and lives in Jacksonville, Florida, has $75,000 in student-loan debt, a fact that's made worse by him not having earned his degree yet.

He's been trying to finish school and pay off the debt since his early twenties. When he was twenty-two, he joined the Florida Army National Guard because the guard said that if he served six years, the government would pay up to $50,000 of his debt. At that point he'd gotten his associate's degree at St. Johns River State College in Orange Park, Florida, and was planning to continue on to get his bachelor's in finance.

He took a break to join the guard, both because he thought it was smart to clear out his debt before taking on more, but also because he was tired of school. Charles is straightforward and honest, even if it means criticizing himself, which he sometimes does harshly. "I'm a shitty student," he often says.

Charles is white and comes from a family with a military background. His father and brother both served. His dad was in the navy. His brother was in the army. "Every male in my family was in [the military], and you fall back on that," he says. At the time, the infantry unit he signed up for was being sent to Kuwait to do convoy missions between Kuwait and Iraq. Charles wanted to go too, but the unit was already deployed when he completed basic training, so he ended up in rear detachment, the group that stays behind and supports the deployed soldiers from afar. "I joined the army to get deployed," he says. "It's in the back of my mind that I don't have the same experience that those who were deployed do. It irks me a little bit. I don't feel like a full-fledged veteran."

Two years later, Charles failed a physical fitness test, which meant the guard wouldn't pay any of his debt—a rule Charles says he didn't know about when he signed up.

Even so, Charles isn't totally down on the experience, which he calls the "best worst time in my life." He's also optimistic about one day earning his degree and getting his debt to zero, though he hasn't made much progress since his early twenties. He's two semesters away from finishing his bachelor's and hopes to be done in about a year, but it's been hard for him to motivate himself to go to class and study.

What keeps him positive is not dwelling. It's not that he ignores reality. He acknowledges his failures, but then he wants to talk about something else. He often says, "But, hey, that's life," before changing topics.

"I just try to do the best I can," he says. "I don't always do that, but you know, hey, just keep on moving."

In addition to going to school, he works full-time as a mortgage loan officer at a bank, where he's paid on commission, which means he doesn't have a steady income. His monthly pay can span a big range, anywhere from $1,800 to $10,000, so even though he plans to pay all of his bills each month, if his earnings are low, he has to roll some of them over to the next month.

He's working toward his finance degree at Florida State College at Jacksonville. Each semester, he signs up for classes and tells himself that he has to go this time. He needs to finish school. But, more often than not, he drops out, usually because he feels overwhelmed by trying to do both his job and go to school, or sometimes just because it's too much of a hassle for no immediate reward—he'd rather be at home, and he doesn't need a degree for his job, anyway.

That is true for now, but it's also shortsighted, as he acknowledges. He wants to get promoted at the bank—not having his bachelor's hinders that. He's told himself he has to be done with school next year in part because that's when a job at the bank that requires a degree is going to be open. The person who has it is retiring, and Charles told his bosses he wants it. "I have made it very clear," he says.

Already, he hasn't gotten a few jobs he's interviewed for at the bank and believes he was turned down because he doesn't have a degree. No one came out and told him that, but "the other candidates had MBAs," he says.

———

Tara Westover, the author of *Educated*, a memoir about earning a PhD after being brought up in a Mormon family that shunned formal schooling, wrote in the *New York Times*, "The life I live now is not the life I was born to. I was propelled up to it, and the motor that powered my ascent was a university education."

That's the ideal of college. It's an opportunity to transcend whatever life parameters seemed set for you—whether it was staying in your hometown, having the same job as your parents, or not reaching for an uncertain career, like becoming an artist or starting a company.

My parents were in the first generations of their families to go to college. They were from the same town, Sheboygan, Wisconsin, and their fathers both worked at the leather tannery, one on the factory floor and the other in personnel. My parents used their degrees to get professional jobs. My dad began his career as an officer in the air force and my mom was a teacher. My mom often told me that she got to go to college only because her older sister had insisted on going. She had to fight my grandfather, who didn't want to send a girl to school.

Today, bypassing college and going straight into the workforce is virtually nonexistent. "There's even a lot of risk of only completing a couple of years of college, as opposed to finishing a bachelor's degree," says Laurence Steinberg, an expert on adolescent development and professor of psychology at Temple University in Philadelphia.

There was never any question I was going to college, although I was scared enough to leave home that I cried when my parents got me luggage for Christmas. I didn't have to take out any loans either. My parents and some small scholarships paid for my tuition at the University of Texas at Austin.

I also never thought college would provide me with a pathway to a life I wasn't already on the way to. It didn't seem like a springboard. It was more like a predetermined way I'd be spending a block of time after high school. That's not to say that I didn't set my future career and self in motion during these years. I made my first attempts at sharing my writing and learned to deal with criticism. One professor rejected a draft of a story, writing on my paper, "You need to be pushed." I met friends I never would have in my hometown, who took me out of my bubble and introduced me to sushi, Ani DiFranco, and not automatically smiling when a guy told me I'd look prettier if I did.

"Has college lost its transformative power?" Westover wrote. "Put simply, no, it hasn't. We live in a knowledge economy, and human capital has never been more valuable."

But that doesn't mean that everyone should have to get—and pay a substantial amount for—a degree on the way to adulthood. The demand for a college degree wasn't driven by innovation or technical need, writes sociologist Tressie McMillan Cottom in *The Credential Society*, a study of the expansion of schooling in twentieth-century America. It was a product of social pressures. People in power made young people feel like they needed a degree, no matter how much it cost.

And so what once guaranteed economic mobility became what a high school degree was for previous generations: a status that made you a respectable adult. Completing a college education was what you had to do before living any more of your life.

But even as a college degree has become just another box to check, it's not equally likely that everyone who sets out to graduate will. Whether you do is largely determined by your parents' income. Seventy-seven percent of children born into the top income quartile will earn a degree by age twenty-four, but for the bottom quartile that number is only 9 percent.

Blacks and Latinos are less likely to have family wealth, and even as they're catching up to white people when it comes to going to college, they aren't getting degrees at the same rate, in part because of the increasing cost. In 2019, about 40 percent of white people age twenty-five and older had a bachelor's degree or more, compared to 26 percent of Black and 19 percent of Hispanic people, according to data from the Current Population Survey.

In other words, the people who were already at the top, who are responsible for hiring choices and dictating that these degrees were necessary in the first place, are also the most likely to get them, benefit from them, and stay at the top.

"The implications are clear: The education system isn't transforming the lives of those who need it most," Westover wrote. "It is dispensing ever more opportunity to those who need it least."

———

Charles lives with his boyfriend, Matt, in a house they co-own. His boss at the bank kept telling him that if he wanted to be serious about selling mortgage loans to other people, he needed to have one of his own.

The house cost $240,000. It was built in 1926 and is two stories, with a broad front porch and an equally expansive balcony. Charles couldn't get the mortgage on his own. He didn't make enough money. And even if he could have, his interest rate would have been high because his credit isn't great. In addition to his student loans, he has credit card and car bills, which, some months, he hasn't paid. So Matt, who he's been dating for seven years, cosigned the loan with him.

Charles used $14,000 from his 401(k) for the down payment and closing costs, which he knows is risky. If he quits his job, he has to pay it back quickly. But he doesn't plan on leaving the company and was proud of starting the retirement fund in the first place. That way he could borrow from himself.

They also have a roommate, who has the top floor to himself; he contributes $500 to the monthly mortgage of $1,890. He's a friend of Matt's, and sometimes they go out to clubs at night, but Charles usually stays home, since they don't leave until ten or eleven. He would rather the roommate wasn't there at all, that it was just Matt and him. "Sometimes you want your own space, you know what I mean?" he says. "But you have to bring in others to help offset the cost."

At his job when he's talking with clients about getting mortgages, he thinks about his own struggle to get one. Not everyone he meets with gets approved, and when he has to tell people they're not qualified he does it tactfully. "I'm not telling you 'No,'" he says to them. "I'm telling you 'Not right now,' so let's figure out how to get you there."

Matt works at a nonprofit that oversees children in foster care, and he's also in school, trying to finish a master's of social work at Florida State. When he and Charles are both taking classes, they do their homework together at the dining room table.

Charles had dropped out of his fall classes but reenrolled for the new year, to start in January. When he did, he texted Matt immediately. "Yay good job," Matt wrote back.

In the mornings, Charles heads to work in jeans and a T-shirt. Matt wears a suit and tie because he usually has to go to family court. They joke about who's working harder.

"Here I am saving the children," he says.

"Well, I'm saving the American dream," Charles retorts.

Charles tends to be impetuous, a trait that is balanced by his being extremely easygoing about whatever happens because of his whims. One weekend he decided he couldn't stand looking at the textured walls in his and Matt's bedroom anymore. They made him think of the cheap apartment his dad moved to for the year his parents were separated when he was ten. It was a two-bedroom apartment with the same walls, and one of the bedrooms was completely empty.

I'll change it out and install drywall, he thought. *I'll be done in a weekend.* Instead, he tore out all the walls, then decided the ceiling should go too, and that they should also install new light fixtures. "That's how I usually do stuff," he says. "I think, *Oh, this will be super easy*, and then I do the hardest thing possible." He hasn't finished the project, and their bedroom has been in disarray for weeks.

Another time, he booked a vacation to Montreal for Matt and him. They go to Disney World in Orlando once or twice a year but haven't traveled anywhere farther in three years. The flights to Montreal were cheap, $305 each, and Charles thought that was such a good deal, he bought them immediately. Then he remembered that he'd lost his passport. He had to pay extra to have a new one rushed to him, so "maybe that wasn't such a good deal after all," he says.

―――

By my early thirties, I'd been living in New York City since my midtwenties, focused mostly on my career as a writer, the one thing I was absolutely sure I wanted.

I wasn't living anything like the fifties model I'd envisioned, but I hadn't forgotten it. I thought that after I solidified my career and my finances, I'd be ready to get married and have children. I thought this even though I was terrified of the compromises I might have to make. What if my theoretical husband wanted to leave New York? How would I balance working with taking care of my theoretical children? Still, I told myself that once I felt secure in my work, I'd be ready to build the rest of what I thought my life should look like from there. Some part of me thought it would happen automatically, as if all the momentum I needed to fill out the rest of my list would come from hitting my professional stride.

I was working at a men's magazine called *Details*. Like so many other magazines, it no longer exists. But in addition to working there, I wrote for other magazines, newspapers, and websites. I was working all the time, trying to get editors to assign me stories, writing those stories, then chasing the next story an editor might assign me. I loved doing this, but I also loved how each time I got a new assignment or had a story published, I felt like I was getting somewhere. I was fortifying this career that I wanted, turning it into a fixed point, something solid that I could then swing the rest of my life around.

I also always felt like I needed more money to spend on my two favorite things—hanging out with friends and buying clothes—but also to save. I was trying to reach some amount that made me feel more secure, although I didn't know what number I was aiming for. In addition to working at *Details* and writing stories for other places, on Sundays, I was a researcher at *Sports Illustrated*, where they paid me $22 an hour to verify that writers had gotten all the facts right in their stories. These were long days. I often didn't get home until after 1:00 a.m. (then had to turn around and go to my job at *Details* on Monday). But I loved being in this office, surrounded by the writers, editors, and words that all seemed to have more heft than a lot of other places I worked because of the history of the magazine. Plus, we had TVs in our offices, and they gave us bagels in the morning and a catered dinner at night. But even with this extra money, I still had—and used—a credit card that my parents paid the bill for.

I got a new job, as a reporter at the *Daily*, a newspaper made only for electronic tablets that was supposed to revolutionize how people read the morning paper (it didn't and also no longer exists). Now, I was making enough money that I felt like I could quit my Sunday job at *Sports Illustrated* and give back the credit card my parents paid for, which I did with little tears in my eyes. I was also getting a lot of story pitches accepted, some at places I'd been trying to write for my whole career. When I read an email on my phone from a *New Yorker* editor saying yes to an idea I'd sent her, I was so excited I started running on the sidewalk.

"We'd like you to give it a try," she wrote.

I had a boyfriend, but he lived across the country. We had a lot of discussions about how we could be in the same place. He wanted me to move to him, and I wanted him to move to me, but we were also okay leaving our living situations as they were and letting our careers be our priority, at least for now.

By the time I was thirty-three, I'd worked my way to my first high-up position on a magazine masthead, at *Women's Health*. I was a senior editor and psyched about the word "senior" being in my title. I got to make real decisions at the magazine, and the job paid me enough money that I could save some. This was the grounding I was looking for.

Then one Wednesday, right after lunch during what felt like an ordinary workday, my boss called.

"Could you come up to the conference room?" she asked.

When I got there, a woman I'd never seen before said she was from Human Resources and asked me to sit. Before I had my butt fully in the chair, she said, "Your position is being eliminated." I was wearing fake leather pants and a sweater with holes in it, an outfit that made me immediately self-conscious. How stupid had I been to think I was a professional with a stable career? They gave me some papers, and I went back to my office and tried not to cry as I looked around for what I wanted to take with me immediately. I grabbed a giant bag of yogurt-covered pretzels I'd bought earlier that week to have as a snack at my desk, which only made me feel more ridiculous and despondent. Then I walked out of the building into a clear, sunny spring day and thought, *My life is ruined.*

All I'd worked for had been taken away in a conference room in less than five minutes.

It only got worse when, on the street, I called my parents to tell them what happened. My dad answered the phone and, after hearing the news, said, "Well, what are you going to do? Do you have a plan?"

I didn't, and in that moment, I felt like I didn't have anything. I thought my career was gone, as was my financial security, and that I was back to the start of trying to put together my life. The one thing I'd been sure about was gone, and since I'd been building everything on that, I didn't have anything else.

I remember crying to my boyfriend after I got fired, "How am I going to get maternity leave now?" even though I wasn't actually sure I wanted to have kids—that's how hamstrung I was by this life order I'd set up for myself and my belief that after I had anchored my career, I would be comfortable deciding on everything else.

My life is nothing like I expected, I thought.

———

Yasin told his relatives—his parents and brothers, as well as his aunts, uncles, and cousins—he was quitting his banking job to start his own company. He's close with all of them. They have a family text chain where they send hundreds of messages a day.

He didn't get the knee-jerk support he wanted. Most of them

didn't understand why he wasn't staying in banking. Even now that it's been a few years, and he's had some success on his own, many of them still think what he did is slightly crazy. "It's not like I'm walking away with five million dollars in my pocket at this point," Yasin says. "Until I have that scenario, it's going to look like I made the wrong move to them."

His father was the most understanding and encouraging. It made sense: he'd wanted to have his own business too and spent most of Yasin's childhood building companies, trying to keep one of them profitable.

Yasin reveres his father, both for his work ethic and for how intelligent he is. "He's a genius," he says. "I never want to be as smart as my father. It's almost too much." His dad graduated at the top of his class from Middle East Technical University in Ankara, Turkey; Yasin calls it the MIT of the Middle East. Yasin's father came to the United States thinking he was going to get a job working in petroleum engineering. After doing that for a few years, he planned to go back to Turkey and run for political office. But the job never materialized. He remained in the United States, but instead of starting his career as an engineer, worked menial jobs as a dishwasher, a cook, and a limo driver.

Eventually Yasin's father and uncle bought two limousines and started their own limousine-rental company. When that failed, they bought two restaurants. Later, they had a lunch truck, then a bread-and-pastry distribution business. "He took the hustle he had, and he and my uncle created some businesses out of it, but you'd never read about them in an *Inc.* article," Yasin says.

Yasin doesn't rush to speak. If he's trying to figure out what to do about something, he prefers to sit and think about it for as long as he needs to. Sometimes he pauses for so long before answering questions that it seems like he isn't going to respond at all.

"My father doesn't have an entrepreneur success story," he says. "But I think he has the typical entrepreneur story, which is you roll with the punches of life. You get bumps. You get bruises. And sometimes you're poorer than when you began. That's the very typical story when it comes to being an entrepreneur, especially an immigrant entrepreneur."

Still, he's inspired by his father's intensity and how much he sacrificed. "I saw him work himself down to the bone," he says. "I have that similar disease, and I don't mind it."

That's what keeps him up until 3:00 a.m. working on budgeting spreadsheets. That's what made him able to get on his laptop at his family's thirty-person Thanksgiving dinner to monitor the app for a few hours, even though it's his favorite holiday and everyone else was being loud, cracking jokes, and having fun. "They gave me the eye like, *I hope you're okay,*" he says.

———

At the end of the year, Charles was expecting a $15,000 bonus and anticipating what he was going to use the money for. "I was like, *I'm going to pay off X, Y, and Z,*" he says. But then he found out that he didn't earn a bonus after all. He'd signed up enough mortgage customers for the year but didn't get high enough ratings from those customers. He left work, went home, and turned on the TV.

"I was so pissed," he says. "I was like, *I'm just going to sit here and pout.* There's that sense in your thirties, you're supposed to be freer. You're growing into yourself more. You're really establishing your career. But that financial monkey is on your back. It's still haunting many of us to where we feel like we can't get to that point."

A few weeks later, though, a hiring manager at his bank called. He wanted Charles to apply for an open position that would be a promotion. Plus, he'd be paid salary *and* commission. The job would be perfect except for the fact that it's in Atlanta, a five-hour drive from Jacksonville, Matt, and the house they own together.

The hiring manager called Charles around noon, but Charles didn't want to say anything to Matt until they could talk in person that evening. When he walked in the house, he made a weird face.

"Uh-oh, what happened?" Matt said. "Did you get fired?"

"The exact opposite," Charles told him.

They talked about the job and Charles moving and decided that if he gets it, Matt would stay in Jacksonville to finish his master's degree, and they'd be long-distance. Charles would come home on weekends. "Of course it will be hard being apart," he says. "But we can navigate that, and he did recognize the financial aspect. It sucks that our whole lives are bent on getting in the best financial position."

The next step is for Charles to interview with the hiring manager and the hiring manager's boss, which he feels confident about, although he did hear that the hiring manager called other candidates besides him. He estimates that his chances at getting the job are "50-50, if not 75-25."

"I don't want to say that it's a guarantee that I have this position because nothing in life is a guarantee," he says, but he's already preparing to move. He withdrew from the six classes he was registered to take in the summer, which pushes his graduation another semester. In the fall, he plans to reenroll in classes he can take online from Atlanta, but right now he thinks it's important for him to be able to concentrate on the new job if he gets it. He knows that not having a degree could keep him from getting it, but hopes the hiring committee likes him enough to overlook that blip on his résumé. "I could screw up the interview, but I don't think I will," he says. "It's just me telling my story. I haven't obtained my degree yet, but it's a journey. I think they could appreciate that. I'll just have to do my best and blow them away."

———

Charles didn't get the job. The hiring manager called to tell him they weren't going to bring him in for the final round of interviews. He didn't say it was because Charles didn't have a degree. He said it was because he didn't have enough experience hiring and managing employees.

After he hung up the phone, Charles started to cry. Previously, the hiring manager, who is in his late thirties, told him that he saw a lot of himself in Charles, like how he was always hustling, but people weren't giving him a chance to move up. "Well, if you see a lot of yourself in me, give me the damn opportunity," Charles says.

He was so mad that he left the office and worked from home for the next week. Then he booked a vacation to London. "I needed a break," he says. "I just picked it randomly." A friend was supposed to come with him, but he bailed, so Charles was by himself, which he didn't mind. He's not shy about going places alone or talking to strangers. One of the things he wanted to do was go to afternoon tea, but everywhere he called was booked, so one day while he was out sightseeing, he decided to walk into the Berkeley Hotel in Knightsbridge to see if they could fit him in. They could.

"I rolled up with my short shorts and button-up shirt, with the ladies in their dresses, and had finger sandwiches," he says.

Another day, he went to St Pancras Brasserie, a restaurant known for having the longest champagne bar in Europe, and started chatting with one of the servers, who invited him to a cookout the staff was having later that day. He went and had a great time.

When he returned to Jacksonville, he told himself to stop being hurt about not getting the job. "I couldn't stay in my feelings for too long," he says. "I had to pick up and move on."

He also reenrolled in school and is taking a marketing class and a banking one, even though, "I'm over it," he says. "I just want to be done." Because he's been working in the banking industry for the past eight years, none of what he's learning in school is new to him, which is another reason school always comes last.

Now, he procrastinates starting his homework until late at night, so he'll be on his laptop at 11:00 p.m. in bed. Matt will look at him like, *Can you go to sleep already?*

———

Charles's dad also works in real estate. He forwarded Charles a job opening for the head of business development at a construction firm and asked Charles to pass it on to his colleagues. Charles couldn't apply because he wasn't qualified: the posting said applicants needed a bachelor's degree.

But Charles didn't send it to anyone. Instead, he decided to take a risk. He was tired of getting passed over for jobs at the bank. The owner of the construction firm was an acquaintance of his. Maybe he wouldn't care that Charles didn't have a degree, despite what the posting read. He wrote him an informal email: *Hey, I don't really think I'm the right person for this job, but just wanted to chat with you about it.*

The boss said they should meet and, when they did, asked him why he didn't think he would be good for the job.

"I don't have a degree," Charles said.

"No?" the boss said.

"I mean, I'm still working toward it," Charles said.

"That's fine," the boss said.

He asked Charles to come in for another interview and another one after that, and, each time, Charles felt like he had to explain why he didn't have a degree. "I'm still working on it," he'd say. "It's been a long time."

Finally the boss said, "Stop apologizing. You're working on it. That's all that really matters."

After six interviews, one of which was Charles and Matt having dinner with the boss and his wife, Charles got the job.

It doesn't pay as much as the bank, but because it's a smaller company, there's more opportunity for him to stand out, be promoted to a bigger position and, consequently, earn more. Leaving the bank also means he has to pay back the money he borrowed from his 401(k) to buy his house, but he can't right now, so he's going to take the penalty. A financial adviser would tell him not to, but he's going to do it anyway.

Charles envisions becoming a partner at the construction firm someday, something he told his boss before he accepted the job. To make that happen, though, he knows he has to finish his degree, and possibly go on for an MBA after that, all of which he's excited to do.

In the meantime, he continues to be uncomfortable not having his bachelor's. At a work event, he started talking to an older man who asked him if he was from Jacksonville, and after Charles said he was, asked him if he'd graduated from college.

"I think his assumption was most people native to Jacksonville do not," Charles says.

Charles lied and told him that he'd graduated from the

University of North Florida, the school that has the MBA program he hopes to be accepted to after finishing his undergraduate degree. Later, he started talking to a younger guy who asked what school he went to. He lied again.

"I graduated from the University of North Florida," he said.

"I hate myself for doing it," Charles says, "but felt it was easiest right then and there."

In reality, he might finish his bachelor's in another year, after this semester and six more credits, but even if he does, "it still will not be my biggest accomplishment in life, not even close," he says. "I see it as a means to an end, nothing more."

CHAPTER TWO

Leaving Home

———————

I was totally the person who was like, "Everything is terrible," and "I'm awful," and "Life sucks" because nothing worked out the way it was supposed to.

—SALLY

Sally never expected to find herself back in her parents' house. But at thirty years old, she was living with them, in the bedroom her sisters shared growing up, in Queens, New York, trying to figure out what to do next and why her plan had fallen apart. She hadn't gone to Paris on a whim. She knew the city. She had thought she had a place to stay. She should have had enough money. But nothing had worked out.

A few years before the move, she never would have thought she would have been in Paris by herself. Sally was born in the Dominican Republic and immigrated to the United States with her parents and two younger sisters when she was three. Her parents married in their midtwenties, and Sally thought she would get married around the same age. She'd fallen in love with her college boyfriend, at Stony Brook University on Long Island, and they had gotten engaged. At the time, Sally already wanted to live in Paris. She had dreamed of doing so since her first trip there as a teenager, when she'd been immediately entranced by the city. She learned French and had traveled there two more times, once with her fiancé. But her fiancé never wanted to live anywhere other than New York. Sally thought he might change his mind, and in the meantime, they'd have their wedding. "I was like, *Oh, okay, I'm going to get married, and it's going to be cool*," Sally says.

Marriage was the start of her adult life, and she was willing to put aside her dream of living in Paris to stick with the plan and make sure it worked.

Then she and her fiancé broke up. They were fighting a lot, mostly about him being distant, and also about money. Sometimes Sally can downplay her emotions, especially when she's reacting to something negative that happened, and ten years after she and her fiancé ended their engagement, she's casual about the decision. They talked about how if they were already married, they would go to therapy and figure out how to communicate better, "but because we were just engaged, it was easy to be like, 'Well, this isn't working, so whatever, okay, I guess we're going to do something else now,'" she says.

Still, she admits, "it was a terrible time in my life." She was letting go of her fiancé, their partnership, and how she saw her future.

She didn't decide to go to Paris immediately. She went to work as usual. She worked in digital marketing at *Latina* magazine, but she was sad and unmotivated every day. Maybe everything felt heavier because she was mourning the end of her relationship, but she kept imagining what her career would look like if she stayed in New York and continued this career path, and hated the trajectory she saw. She pictured herself plodding along as a manager for another year or so, then being promoted to director, and maybe eventually being the boss. She didn't want to do any of that. So she quit and bought a ticket to Paris. She planned to be there for three months, a test run for moving permanently.

When she got off the plane, she remembered the trip she had taken there with her former fiancé and how they'd fought for most of it. He wanted her to speak French for him, but she hates translating for other people. As a kid, she had to do that for her Spanish-speaking mom and dad at parent-teacher meetings and at doctors' appointments. "It gave me a lot of anxiety because it was like our survival depends on me being able to translate what this person is saying," she says. "Anytime I'm expected to translate for someone I shut down."

She was glad to be there without him.

She stayed with a friend in the 6th arrondissement, and life in Paris was exactly how she fantasized it would be. She spoke French, went on walks with friends, hung out in cafés, and visited the Musée d'Orsay and the Père Lachaise, the cemetery where Jim Morrison and Oscar Wilde are buried, and one of Sally's favorite places in the city.

She returned to the United States, and after saving some money from hosting writing workshops and working for a college-prep company editing students' admission essays, decided to go back to Paris—this time, on a one-way ticket. Another friend said she could stay with him for free as long as she needed, and she hoped to host a writing retreat in Paris, so she'd have some income if it took her a long time to find a job. She advertised the retreat on her blog, and a few readers responded that they wanted to attend. She thought she'd planned as well as she could.

When she got off the plane in Paris, she felt great. She had a sense of being at home whenever she was there. And now she was excited to make the city her real home. But after only a few weeks, her friend needed to move out of his apartment; Sally would have nowhere to stay. She tried to book an Airbnb for cheap—she hadn't found a job and was running low on money—and instead found one where she could stay for free, in exchange for helping the host edit the book he was working on. Sally didn't let herself be nervous about the arrangement. This was a way to remain in Paris. "I was mostly like, 'Oh thank goodness, a bed,'" she says. "That was all I needed at that point."

But a few days into the arrangement, the owner of the Airbnb woke her up and told her she had to go. He decided that he didn't want her to stay for free anymore; he was going to charge for the room again.

She did the only thing she could think of. She rolled her suitcase across the Seine to the Père Lachaise cemetery. On her previous trips to Paris, she'd gone there to honor the dead and, at the same time, be thankful she was alive.

This time though, she sat among the tombstones and trees,

with her suitcase next to her, and sobbed until dark, when the cemetery closed.

———

The night after Sally was kicked out of the Airbnb, she booked a bed in a hostel but knew that wasn't a long-term solution. She only had enough money for a few more nights at the hostel. She tried to confirm with the people who had wanted to attend her writing retreat that they were still coming but didn't hear back from them.

She didn't want to call her mom. Sally hesitates about letting her know when things in her life are going badly; she fears she will make her feel worse about what's happening. But eventually she talked to her, "probably because I knew she would do anything to help," she says. She told her best friend and her two sisters too. Everyone sent her what money they could, when they could. It was usually enough for only one more night at the hostel, so every morning Sally would check out, store her suitcase in the luggage room, walk around the city with her backpack, and hope that by the end of the day she got enough money to check in again. The staff never asked her what was going on, but Sally kept wondering, *What do they think my life is?*

On paper, what she was doing wasn't that harrowing. She was spending her days walking around with a backpack while waiting for people who loved her to send money. But it felt worse in her head. Every day, as she walked around Paris, she was anxious and scared. She could barely breathe. "It was such a traumatic experience," she says.

She did this routine for about a month. That was how much time it took for her mom to get together enough money to buy her a plane ticket back to the United States. Sally doesn't know the specifics of how her mom raised the cash—she never asked her; they never talk about money—but she thinks her mom saved her own money and asked family and friends for donations.

When Sally left Paris, she ended up in a place she thought she'd never be going back to: her parents' house in Queens.

———

The majority of thirtysomethings whose stories are in this book moved back home with their parents at some point in their twenties or thirties. One did it after a breakup. Another after his wife lost her job. One was trying to save money to buy her own place.

The fact that out of a random sample of young adults, most of them had returned to their parents' homes after they thought they were gone for good is consistent with what the national statistics show: In 2014, for the first time, living with one's parents became the most common living arrangement for Americans ages eighteen to thirty-four, overtaking living with a romantic partner. Black and Hispanic young adults are more likely to live at home, but the trend is similar for all major racial and ethnic groups.

The rise in young adults residing with their parents isn't only due to economic instability. The percentage did start to increase during the Great Recession of 2008, but continued to climb well after it was over. By 2018, about twenty-five million adults ages eighteen to thirty-four were living at home, per a Pew Research Center analysis of data from the Census Bureau.

In part, the increase is due to people marrying later—on average, at thirty for men and twenty-eight for women (men are more likely than women to live with their parents). But education, or lack thereof, also affects people's ability to have their own homes. In general, people who have college degrees—and the pay and job security that comes with them—are less likely to stay with their folks. Those who don't are more likely to have trouble finding work that pays them enough to live independently.

The coronavirus pandemic has only added to the number of young adults returning to their parents, either because of their college campuses closing, prolonged unemployment meaning they could no longer pay rent, or simply wanting the emotional security, and in some cases childcare, gained from being near family. A recent analysis of government data by the real-estate website Zillow indicated that about 2.9 million adults moved in with a parent or grandparent in the spring of 2020, if college students were included.

But, despite how common this arrangement is, there is still a lot of fretting about it. We picture the full-grown adult getting high on the couch while Mom scurries around doing the laundry.

We see Zach Galifianakis playing the man-child Alan in *The Hangover*. We think, *Isn't it time for them to get their own place?*

Other countries, like Italy and South Korea, don't see it this way. Unlike in America, where you're supposed to turn eighteen and never look back, there, living with your parents is the norm until you marry, and even after that, the new couple might stay until their finances are more secure. Moving out before then would be an insult to the people who raised you.

The judgment that living with your parents is not okay comes from the fear that delaying leaving home sets back your psychological development, says Laurence Steinberg. But he's skeptical of the doomsday thinking. He says what you're doing when you're residing with Mom and Dad matters more than the fact that you're living with them. For example, are you going to medical school in San Francisco, where housing prices are preposterous?

"There's no reason that kind of scenario should lead to being less mature," he says. "It's just a convenient and money-saving option. Just because someone is living with his or her parents doesn't tell you anything without knowing how they spend their time. We have a view of that in the United States of something that's abhorrent or indicative of problematic development, but that's only because we're not used to seeing it."

When Lucy Huber and her husband, Matt, finished school and moved to her parents' retirement community (where most residents were sixty and older) on Dataw Island in South Carolina, they thought they'd be there for a few weeks. They moved in August, and "I remember a friend invited us to her wedding in

September, and I was like, 'I don't know if I can go because I don't know where I'm going to be living,'" Lucy says.

She and Matt met in college and had both been in school a long time. She got a master's in creative writing after her bachelor's, which took seven years total, and Matt was in school for three years after she finished, earning a master's in chemistry and a PhD in chemical biology after his undergraduate degree. As Matt's graduation approached, they were twenty-nine and thirty and optimistic. They'd gotten married a few months before and figured by then he'd have a job—and they'd have a new city to move to.

When that hadn't happened by August, they didn't know what to do or have any savings to do anything with. So they ended up in the guest room of Lucy's parents' retirement cottage. It was filled with things Lucy thought she left behind: her childhood rocking horse, a box of notes from middle school, her high school yearbooks.

At first, living in the retirement community was fun. During the day they went to the gym, where they ignored Fox News blaring. At sunset, they had cocktails on the porch overlooking the golf course, and, after dinner, they watched *Wheel of Fortune* with her parents. They set up working hours, getting up at the same time and being in front of the computer until five, even if neither of them had much to do. "We both felt this mix of guilt that we weren't where we thought we would be, and also that we needed to work harder, otherwise it wasn't going to work, and we were terrified we'd be stuck there forever," Lucy says.

But after a few months, they started to fight. It was around the same time Lucy turned thirty. Her birthday, eating cake in her parents' kitchen while living with them in the retirement community, wasn't how Lucy imagined this birthday ("You think, *I'm going to have this big party at my house that I own*," she says). Pretending to be retired before they'd even started their careers no longer seemed charming. Instead, Lucy felt like she'd done no growing up at all. Her parents shopped for them, and she had to ask to borrow the car. "It feels weird to live with your parents when you're thirty, especially with your husband," she says. "Obviously there's some things I don't want my parents to be around for. We hadn't even been married a full year."

She kept thinking, *How is it possible that my husband has a PhD, and we've done everything we're supposed to do, and here we are living with my parents and we have no money? We have nothing. If we are here, how do people not end up here? We had, not every advantage, but a lot of advantages, and it still was hard and we struggled, and we ended up living in a retirement community.*

But even as she was ready to bolt anywhere but there, she was grateful for the time with her parents. She and her mom had coffee together in the morning before everyone else woke up. Matt joined her dad's Ping-Pong team. Eventually they left—Matt got a job in Boston—and she was sad to go.

"As much as I felt restless being there, it was also comfortable," she says. "My parents were taking care of us, and even though it was frustrating, it was easy. In a way I was sad to leave because I felt scared of having to start a life for real."

———

Marcus moved back in with his parents after he graduated from college. He was trying to be responsible. He had $9,000 in student-loan and credit card debt, but his job doing data entry paid only $19,500 a year, barely enough to cover the minimum payments. He told himself he could survive in his childhood bedroom in Trinity, Texas, a small town of less than three thousand residents outside of Houston, until he cleared his loans and got a better-paying job.

He lasted three months. After four years of freedom at college, he hated being in what he called "Home Alcatraz." His breaking point was when his mom found an open online chat with a girl he had been talking to and saw that instead of taking a trip to Dallas with his friends like he said, he'd taken a cross-country flight to see the girl.

Marcus moved into a studio apartment *with* the girl, but didn't make enough money to cover his debt and pay rent, so he applied for a $10,000 loan to consolidate his debt. He thought the consolidation company would give him a new monthly payment. Instead, they mailed him a $10,000 check. When Marcus saw it, "I just went completely crazy," he says.

Marcus has been criticized for not being introspective enough, mostly by girlfriends, and he does tell the story of the spending spree that followed him getting this check more like a stand-up comedian than a guy whose life was about to be derailed because of it. In thirty-six hours, he and his girlfriend spent the entire check and then some on clothes, liquor, "name-brand name brands," a $3,000 flat-screen television, and a $13,000 used Toyota Camry. "It had really big rims," Marcus says.

Marcus had tripled his debt, and his girlfriend didn't stay to help with the fallout. She broke up with him to move to New York to pursue her modeling career full-time. He didn't want his friends to know about his debt, so he took side jobs so he could still spend money while he was paying it. He sold phones at AT&T, manned the overnight desk at a hotel, and assembled computers at the Dell warehouse.

"Everyone thought I was doing fine," he says. "They thought, like, *He made it.* I was always out there stunting. Anytime anyone saw me, I was always making it rain. They must have thought, *You're doing it. You're doing the American dream.*"

Right before he turned thirty, he sent his final payment. He'd been trying to get rid of his debt for eight years, but after he did, he didn't know what to do with himself.

His new girlfriend asked him, "Shouldn't you be celebrating?"

Marcus didn't want to. Paying his debt had given him something concrete to go after, but now that he was done, he felt lost. His life didn't look like how he thought it would after he graduated from college. He thought he'd have a well-paying job, which he did, but he also thought he'd have a wife, a house, and kids, which he didn't. Had it been a mistake to ignore those things while he was busy paying his debt? He felt anxious and out of control. He worried: *What's next?*

———

A lot of us are certain we're screwing up adulthood. The writer Kelly Williams Brown came up with the term "adulting" when she was feeling like her life was completely unmanageable. Everyone around her seemed so focused and accomplished, driven to push themselves more every day, while she never remembered to buy toilet paper and was using mosquito repellent to keep her cat's fleas from biting her. She was sure her life was a disaster and her days weren't the days of an adult.

"I felt so out of control and messy and bad," she says, "and the truth was that, relatively speaking, I really wasn't doing very poorly at all. I was working in the field I had gone to school for. I had a cat, some furniture. It's not like I was feral on the street, but I still really felt like I was just a mess."

She set out to write the book *Adulting: How to Become a Grown-Up in 468 Easy(ish) Steps* to help people like her who wanted to feel like their lives had forward momentum. But when she began asking people she thought were inspirational for their suggestions, "I started to realize that everyone else also felt like they were messes," she says.

Every single person she tried to interview would tell her, "You don't want to talk to me. I'm not a real adult."

"And I would be like, 'You're a surgeon! What are you talking about?'" Williams Brown says.

The book came out in 2013, and since then the word

"adulting" has evolved into a cutesy verb that means performing tasks that seem grown-up, like making a dentist appointment or boiling an egg.

It's on T-shirts: I'M TIRED OF "ADULTING." I'M GOING BACK TO MY PILLOW FORT.

And: ADULTING. /UH-DUHLT-ING/ V. MIMICKING THINGS YOU SEE REAL ADULTS DO IN AN ATTEMPT TO TRICK PEOPLE INTO BELIEVING YOU ARE A SUCCESSFUL ADULT AS WELL.

Saying you're "adulting" has become more of a way to show off, as much as anyone can show off that they're wearing matching socks or making dinner, than a way to soothe the internal ickiness of fearing that you don't have your shit together.

"'Adulting' as a word really annoys me now," Williams Brown says.

But that doesn't mean the unease Williams Brown was trying to tap into isn't at the red-hot center of many of us and, in fact, the people who seem the most like they have secure lives can often feel the least like they do. But unless they express their feelings, it's hard to believe they're not doing better than you.

"We're always going to compare our own lives to our very shallow, uninformed impression of someone else's life because we don't have access to anyone else's interior life," Williams Brown says.

———

Marcus didn't always hate his job. He spent the beginning stretch of his career as an auditor going after bigger and bigger salaries and, at thirty-six, earns "Nine hundred and ninety-three dollars under six figures, not that I'm keeping track," he says. But now that he has a job that pays him well, he wishes he wasn't doing it, dissatisfaction that surprised him. "If you had told my younger self, you'll make six figures and not be happy, I might have slapped myself," he says, "like that doesn't make any sense."

What he wants to do instead is educate young people about how not to get into debt like he did. When he started telling the truth about how much debt he had and what he had to do to repay it, he realized that he liked sharing his story and trying to help others not to repeat it. "I used to be really embarrassed to talk about how I got into $30,000 in debt," he says, "but someone told me representation matters. There aren't a lot of men, particularly Black men, out here telling that story." He has a financial-advice podcast, *Paychecks and Balances,* and gives speeches to groups in their teens and twenties.

That Marcus is African American is something many people he communicates with online as he's promoting his podcast and speaking gigs don't realize until they see him in person. White people often tell him that they didn't expect him to be Black.

"A lot of people are surprised," he says. "They say, 'Oh, you're a Black guy.'" Or if they're African American themselves, they might tell him he's not really Black. Marcus thinks this is in part due to the fact that he grew up in a mostly white suburb and went to a predominantly white college.

"If you wrote down all of the things on a piece of paper that represented my life, you'd think I was an upper-middle-class white guy," he says.

He's attempted to figure out where he fits within his race since high school. Then, perhaps to overcompensate for not feeling Black enough, he wore a medallion on a chain with the words "100% Black."

"I got so much shit, mostly from Black people," Marcus says. "Like, 'You ain't 100 percent Black, you light-skinned mother-fucker.'"

Now, he gets questioned on his race when he talks about how much money he makes. He understands the impulse to do this but pushes back. "How is my experience any different?" he says. "Because at the end of the day when I go to sleep I'm still a Black man, so why do our experiences have to be equal? Why aren't they represented as just experience?"

Instead of being an auditor, Marcus wants to run his financial-education business as a full-time job, but that would mean he'd be working on his own without regular income. It would be a good time to take a financial risk. He doesn't own a house, or have a wife or children, but he can't convince himself to quit his auditing job, no matter how unhappy he is at work. He's scared to give up his monthly paycheck.

"I'm not a walk-away guy," Marcus says. "It's hard for me to tell myself, *Oh, pursue your dreams,* because not all dreams pay." Instead, he uses vacation days for speaking gigs and records the podcast on Saturday mornings (before his friends start waking up around noon and "want to do childish, irresponsible things," that he participates in happily, he says).

His dad doesn't understand why he's searching for more than the job he has. He started his career as a parole officer, advanced to be the chairman of the Texas Board of Pardons and Paroles, and retired with a pension. He tells Marcus, "Why don't you go to work for forty years like I did and chill, then retire and chill some more?"

"But I'm pretty sure there's more to life than that," Marcus says. "Like, I know there's more."

When Marcus started looking for a new job, he was optimistic. Maybe he could find one doing financial speaking or education. After applying to a bunch of those kinds of positions and not hearing back, he thought he could at least get another auditing job that would be a promotion. He went on a couple of interviews but didn't get any offers and, at the same time, became more unhappy at work. He went on vacation with his girlfriend, L, to a jazz festival in Cabo San Lucas, Mexico. It used to be that after he got back from a trip, "I'd have that vacation glow for a nice stretch, where no BS could penetrate that," he says. "But after Mexico, I got back on Tuesday and by Wednesday I was like, 'I need another vacation.'"

At this point he's applied for more than a hundred jobs and is willing to work for any company that wants him. "The way I describe it," he says, "I started off as the picky person on Tinder, and now I'm like, 'Whoever swipes on me is my wife.'" The job in San Antonio that he didn't get was actually a demotion, but Marcus would have done it—it was a way out.

L wants to move to Texas from Chicago to be closer to Marcus, but she doesn't want to live with him until they are engaged. Marcus is a little nervous about her moving for him. He's had some bad relationships in the past. His girlfriend he had during his twenties left him after their shopping spree. Another girlfriend was so jealous of his female friends that she refused to let him hang out with them. He took on another girlfriend's $18,000 debt. "I thought, wrongly, that we would be together forever," he says.

But with L, everything has been going well so far. They've been dating for a year and see each other every month. Marcus likes that she's independent. With other girlfriends, Marcus has paid for everything, but when he and L visit each other she buys her flight or the hotel room. She's an engineer, so they think similarly, both preferring to focus on numbers and data when they make decisions.

He wants them to try their relationship while living in the same place but doesn't know where he's going to get a job. Until he knows what city he is going to live in, she can't leave Chicago. She'd wanted to get to Texas by May, but it was already summer and he hadn't found a new job. Nothing was going how Marcus thought it would, and he was getting increasingly agitated.

L was getting antsy too. She had a birthday; turning a year older prompted her to talk to Marcus about if he wanted to have kids and when. In his early thirties, Marcus had brooded a lot about not having a family and kids, but as he'd gotten older he'd been okay with it. He'd assumed that it would happen, but when it didn't, he stopped thinking about it as much. His mom stopped asking when he'd have kids too.

Then he started dating L and, that year, brought her to his parents' house for Thanksgiving. As they were leaving, Marcus noticed his mom's massive doll collection was gone and asked where it was. "I never thought you'd have kids so I gave it away," she said.

"I put it on the backboard for her," Marcus says, laughing, "and she dunked it in my face."

L's wanting to have kids made Marcus think that he might want to as well. But before they committed to the idea, he wanted to have a job he liked, settle into them both being in the same place, and possibly get married. From where he was at, unable to check off step one—getting a new job—it seemed impossible he could make any of it fall into place. He was in his head and frustrated. "I'm like, 'When?'" he says. "When does this happen?"

———

Beyond living with your parents past a certain age, generally anything that seems like delaying adulthood is seen negatively. Older adults look at younger people and bemoan the fact that they don't have steady jobs, aren't married, or don't have kids. Steinberg explains the main reason for this criticism: supposedly, not taking on these adult roles slows our psychological growth.

"So if we're talking about something like the development of responsibility, if you're not entering in career-related employment until much later, maybe that's slowing people's ability to be responsible," he says. "Or, an analogous argument would be that because you're not getting married, there's some stunting in the development to be intimate with other people."

Steinberg, however, doesn't agree with any of this and sees no evidence that delaying adulthood impacts psychological development. "I think there's a lot of misguided hand-wringing," he says.

Instead, he thinks that there could be benefits to delaying adulthood. Not settling into long-term roles and relationships could lead to a longer period of the brain growing and improving, with new experiences creating new neural pathways (the connections in the brain formed by repeated behaviors that help make us who we are).

During adolescence, studies show the brain changes constantly, what's known as "plasticity." The new experiences you have shake up the brain and help us develop our habits, talents, and emotional responses. This is how we realize we're capable of more than we thought we were, or that there are different ways to go about the world. This stimulation, however, slows as we age. Once we reach adulthood, our brain circuits are mostly set—they can be adjusted slightly, but not completely remade. "No one knows why, but your brain loses a lot of plasticity at that time," Steinberg says.

But if your brain is kept busy with new, not-so-easy-to-conquer experiences for longer, it makes sense that it would keep on developing. And the more time the brain avoids being static, the more likely you are to discover new skills and wants and, in general, evolve and grow. Even in the long term, after the brain is done changing, Steinberg says, having a prolonged period where the synapses proliferate helps the brain react more strongly to inspiring experiences you might have in the future. "So if people are delaying entrances into these adult roles," he says, "but they're immersing themselves in circumstances that are going to be novel and challenging, then it could be advantageous in that they're having a longer period of brain plasticity."

———

In the weeks and months after my job was eliminated, I couldn't find another job and started working on my own as a freelance writer, which meant I no longer had a regular paycheck, company-sponsored health insurance, or an active 401(k). I also no longer had a job that seemed like an actual job. When I'd tell people I was freelancing, their reaction, either implicitly or explicitly, was that I was just waiting until someone offered me a real job.

My boyfriend and I broke up. He wanted me to move to his city, since he was the one who still had a corporate job, but I didn't want to: that seemed like admitting failure, a retreat that I was forced into because I couldn't make my own career happen.

I started to spend a lot of time by myself. In the beginning I was working more than ever, panicked about money, but also grasping for something work-related that would make me feel as centered and capable as I had before I'd been fired.

I did not find it. I was getting assignments from editors, including one for the most substantial and personal piece I'd ever written, but none of it helped me relax. Instead, I felt like I was always in a corner, coiled and ready to spring at whatever opportunity I spotted.

It was exhausting, but it could also be exhilarating. What I hadn't considered about no longer having a corporate job was that I was also no longer in a box. I was doing different kinds of writing than I'd done before, work that I thought was good. I was stretching my skills and getting a buzz like, *I didn't know I could do that*. It wasn't a perfect upswing. I was also unprotected, uncertain, and prone to crying sometimes, especially at the end of the day when the buzz wore off and what I heard in my head instead was, *What am I doing?*

But I also wasn't ready to quit. I kept writing without the security of working for the same place each day and started to feel a lot better about it—and about my life. This happiness would ambush me sometimes, like when I'd be walking down the street and think suddenly, *I want to be doing this*. I could go days feeling good before I'd panic again.

I'd been trying to get to a solid career so I could launch the rest of what I thought my life had to be, but now I had to let that go. I no longer had a precise answer to what I did. It wasn't going to be what would propel me to marriage, buying a home, having children, or simply feeling like an established adult.

I was untethered from the list I thought I was following and existing just as I was. For so long, I'd been forcing this image of what my life had to look like, but then, suddenly I couldn't pretend all of that was around the corner anymore—or that I even wanted it to be.

Psychotherapist Lori Gottlieb wrote in her memoir *Maybe You Should Talk to Someone*, "When the present falls apart, so does the future we had associated with it. And having the future taken away is the mother of all plot twists."

When I separated the strands of what I assumed my life would look like from how it actually did, a surprising thing happened: I felt free.

Around this time I bought myself a cell phone case with a motivational message that read: *What if I fall? / Oh but my darling, What if you fly?*

My best friend, Ruthie, rolled her eyes at it. "But I guess you're going through some stuff," she said, which made me laugh.

I didn't feel like I was flying. Just because I no longer assumed my traditional adulthood would snap into place didn't mean that I wouldn't want one eventually. I might seek a less volatile career. I could want to live in a home that didn't feel temporary. I might want to get married. I could want to have children. I hadn't forgotten what was on my list. But I did sort of feel like I was floating. I wanted to have all kinds of experiences and joys and loves, and I had to figure out what those were for myself.

My thirties weren't going to be about markers but the spaces in between them and who I showed myself to be when things didn't work out, when everything was uncomfortable, and when I tried to go after what I really wanted instead of just looking for somewhere to stop.

———

Today, the idea that you would be washed-up at thirty seems ludicrous, but in the sixties and early seventies, it was a popular sentiment. During the protests against the Vietnam War, and for civil rights and free speech, one of the defining slogans was: "Don't trust anyone over thirty." Anybody over thirty was too old to understand what young people were fighting for. The quote came from the activist Jack Weinberg, a student at UC Berkeley. In 1964, he was arrested for passing out leaflets about the civil rights movement on campus. He worked in the South over the summer and wanted to share with the other students the racial oppression he saw, but the university forbade anyone from handing out political literature.

Officers put Weinberg in the back of a police cruiser, but students surrounded the car, blocking the way out. The crowd grew to thousands of protestors, with the leaders climbing onto the roof of the police car to give speeches (some took their shoes off before they did) while the throng around them sang "We Shall Overcome." Students were allowed to pass Weinberg food and water, as well as empty bottles to pee in. The protest lasted thirty-two hours and kicked off the national free speech movement.

Shortly after Weinberg's arrest, a reporter for the *San Francisco Chronicle* asked him if someone other than students was really in charge of the movement. The reporter speculated that maybe Communists were really leading it.

An irritated Weinberg told him, "We have a saying in the movement that we don't trust anybody over thirty."

"I was being interviewed by this guy," Weinberg told the *Washington Post* in 1970, "and he was, or seemed to be, saying something that was bothering me. He was probing into the question of weren't there outside adults manipulating us. There was the implication of a 'Communist conspiracy.' That was infuriating, so I said the thing about not trusting anybody over thirty as a kind of taunt. I was trying to tell him there weren't any graybeards manipulating us."

A columnist for the *Chronicle* then used the quote in his column. Other journalists reprinted it, and when the activists realized how much this idea bothered the older generation—their time had come and gone; the youth were leading culture now—they began to chant in earnest: "Don't trust anyone over thirty." In Ralph Keyes's book about misquotations, *Nice Guys Finish Seventh*, he wrote, "Before long this became the defining slogan of an era when surly youths were seen as rudely elbowing their parents aside."

Being younger than thirty meant you could be idealistic and unattached; free to follow, and organize your life around, whatever intrigued or inspired you at the moment. Yale psychologist Kenneth Keniston observed these student protests and, more generally, that people in their late teens and early twenties weren't rushing to take on responsibilities in the same way their elders had. There was "a growing minority of postadolescents [who] have not settled the questions whose answers once defined adulthood: questions of relationship to existing society, questions of vocation, questions of social role and lifestyle," he wrote in the *American Scholar* in 1970. Keniston called what was happening unprecedented—previously, this rootlessness had been found only in the "unusually creative or unusually disturbed," he wrote. But today young people "can't seem to 'settle down.'" They have "the feeling of absolute freedom, of living in a world of pure possibilities."

But turning thirty was the end of this opportunity to do whatever you wanted. In 1970, the oldest baby boomers were twenty-four. They transitioned to thirties that looked like they had in previous generations. They got jobs, married, bought houses, and had kids. At least on the surface, they were the same kind of adults their parents had been. In 1971, the novelist John Updike wrote in the novel *Rabbit Redux* about Harry "Rabbit" Angstrom's midlife crisis, "What you haven't done by thirty you're not likely to do."

Once their lives were set, however, thirtysomethings often didn't like being in them. In 1979, divorces hit a historical high point, when 22.6 marriages out of every 1,000 broke up, according to researchers at the National Center for Family & Marriage Research at Bowling Green State University.

Author Gail Sheehy pinpointed this dissatisfaction in her

bestselling book *Passages: Predictable Crises of Adult Life*, which was originally published in 1974.

She noticed it in herself first, when she had her own misgivings with who she was at thirty-five. She'd married at twenty-four, had a daughter four years later, and divorced her husband four years after that. Her daughter was now seven, and Sheehy was a successful magazine writer, but suddenly all of what she was doing didn't seem like enough, as if she'd stopped evolving herself too soon.

"Some intruder shook me by the psyche and shouted: *Take stock! Half your life has been spent*," she wrote in *Passages*. "*What about the part of you that wants a home and talked about a second child?* Before I could answer, the intruder pointed to something else I had postponed: *What about the side of you that wants to contribute to the world? Words, books, demonstrations, donations—is this enough? You have been a performer, not a full participant. And now you are 35.*"

She used her own experience and interviews with 115 middle-class men and women ages eighteen to fifty-five to identify a period in their thirties that she called "the Catch-30," when people suddenly wanted to be more than they were or tear up their life and start over. "I think I was very fortunate," Sheehy told the *Christian Science Monitor*, "in having the profession I do because in part I think every writer who does a book about serious subjects is working out some of their own demons."

Before then, no one had identified that adults—ancient already at thirty!—might be having doubts about their lives. Sheehy gave them a voice and described the agony of suddenly reassessing all that you thought you had been responsible by building in the first place, with real sympathy. The book was on the *New York Times* Best Sellers list for more than three years.

"Men and women alike speak of feeling too narrow and restricted," she told *People* magazine in 1976. "They blame all sorts of things—their choices in their 20s of mates and careers. But what it boils down to is that choices perfectly suited to the 20s are no longer enough. Some inner aspect was left out that is striving to be taken into account . . . Suddenly one is less concerned with what I 'should do' than what I 'want to do.'"

———

Marcus wanted to see a therapist, but he hadn't made an appointment, even after the night he'd been immobile in his parents' hotel room. L was encouraging him to go too. One weekend, he swore to her that he would make an appointment, but he still didn't.

Actually going to therapy meant that he had to admit to himself that he could no longer handle his life, and "I feel like I should be able to," he says. If he had gotten a new job, he would have buried how awful he felt about the future seeming unmanageable. But no one would hire him, and he was becoming increasingly despondent about not being able to plot his life how he wanted. He needed help.

"I need to get over myself," he says. "I could have done this months ago. I don't know why it's hard. I can't put my feet together to walk to the therapist's office."

Then one night, he found himself crying on his couch. He rarely cries. His friends would have freaked out if they'd seen him, but Marcus didn't panic. He just let himself cry and thought, *Maybe I'm not handling this as well as I could.*

After that, he finally made an appointment with a therapist, a woman. "I've gone to male friends on some unrelated things," he says, "and they're just like, *Man up.* I didn't need to hear that right now."

He doesn't know what to expect, but "it can't be worse than what I'm doing, which is nothing," he says. "I'm self-medicating and closing myself off to the world. I'm thinking I'm dealing with it, but it's building over time. I don't know where I'm going to live, where I'm going to work, where me and my girlfriend are going to live. Intellectually I know it's not hopeless, but I am pretty exhausted. I'm like, *It's been almost forty years, and what are we doing here?*"

At her parents' house in Queens, Sally started to think about how she was always planning her life. It was what she did. First, she thought she'd be married and have a corporate job. Then she was going to move to Paris and get away from all of that. But none of her plans had worked. Plans didn't mean things wouldn't fall apart. So she decided to stop. No more plans. She was just going to do what she wanted and trust that it was going to work out in some way, without her attempting to put up any sort of safety net.

"I became bolder," she says. "What did I have to lose?"

One of the first things she did was start dating. She and her ex-fiancé had met in college, so she hadn't dated as an adult. Now she wanted to date widely without any limits on who she was trying to meet or how many guys she would go out with; she just wanted to be open. "I was like, *Well, now I'm free*," she says. "I'm not engaged. This is a very different life than the one I was planning on, so I'm going to date everyone."

She went out with guys she met on the dating site OkCupid, old friends she had always had crushes on, her favorite waiter at her favorite pizza place, and a police officer who came by to investigate a possible break-in at her parents' house. She wanted to have fun getting to know these guys. Turning one of them into her boyfriend wasn't important to her.

"Most of my male friends have seen me naked because we've had sex," she says. "That's how we became friends."

Her mom was watching her date, and at one point, she cornered Sally about the number of guys she was seeing come to pick up her daughter. "Why don't you try meeting one person and hanging out with him for a little longer?" she asked.

In general, Sally is never sure what her mom wants from her. She raised Sally and her two sisters to be independent. She never worked outside the home; "it's not Dominican culture," Sally says. But she didn't want her daughters to have to do the same thing. When they were growing up, she told Sally and her sisters, "I'm not going to teach you to cook because then you'll have to cook for your husband."

Even though her mom didn't want her daughters cooking for their husbands, she did expect them to marry and have children, like she did, but none of them have. Sally's thirty-four now, and her mom tells her that she's too old to have a kid. "I'm like, *That's great*," she says. "I don't ever fully know where she's at. I think it must be challenging to have the desire for us to be married and have kids while also being like, 'Way to go, them,' and being really happy and grateful she raised three daughters who are cool being by themselves."

———

In Queens, Sally began working on another business she'd been dreaming of: she wanted to start a company to assist small-business owners with whatever they needed. She could build business plans. She could help with websites or other marketing. She could answer emails from customers. Or she could do all of those things.

After six months, and signing up a piano teacher and a leadership coach as clients, she had enough money to buy another plane ticket, this time to visit her sisters in California. One lived in Los Angeles, the other in San Francisco. She didn't make any plans beyond, *I'll spend two weeks in San Francisco, two weeks in Los Angeles, and see what happens.*

She'd been to Los Angeles before, but this was the first time she considered that it could be her home—in particular, the jacaranda trees, with their pale blue flowers, made her feel calm and safe. As it got closer to when she was supposed to leave LA, she decided she wasn't going to. She started to establish her life there, which included thinking that she wanted to be in a relationship again. She started musing about who her perfect person might be, using what she liked about who she had dated in the past to figure out her ideal. "I was like, *If I do want a relationship, who the hell do I want to be in a relationship with?*" she says.

She wanted someone creative, but not obsessed with work; kind and chivalrous, but also fine with her opening her own doors and carrying her own bags. This person should be extremely into her, but also have his own interests and passions she wasn't part of. "It was a real Goldilocks situation," she says. "I was looking for someone just right." This person didn't have to be her next fiancé. She wasn't trying to force anything. *I just want one person who's my consistent person*, she thought.

Jay was the first person she went on a date with in LA. They met on a dating app called Coffee Meets Bagel. He's thirty-two, grew up in Detroit, and was working doing postproduction for a movie studio. She liked him enough on the first date to go on a second one, which is when she really started to think he might be the person she was looking for. He wanted to have fun, was open-minded, and "really nice, sweet, and kind," Sally says, "which I don't think are words I would use to describe many of the people I've dated."

After they'd been dating a few months, Sally asked him, "So are you, like, my boyfriend? Just because people keep asking about you, and I don't know how to refer to you. What do you want to do with that?"

He answered her question with a question: "Do you want me to call you my girlfriend?"

"I remember it being very sweet," Sally says.

They'd been dating nine months when Sally's apartment lease ended. Jay said she could stay with him while she looked for another place. She thought it would be a month or two, but after three months she still hadn't found a new apartment. In the meantime, Jay had started thinking about quitting his job at the movie studio to write and direct his own films, which meant he'd be living off savings until he started making money from filmmaking. She needed a place to live; he needed financial support.

"Did you want me to live here?" Sally asked him.

"I think that would make sense," he said.

Jay quit his job, and Sally started paying the rent for the entire apartment, which she could do since she was starting to make more money from her various projects. Sometimes, she worries that her income isn't sustainable—and feels bad for always changing what she's doing (her sister now co-runs her business with her—they have six clients, so that occupies most of her time, so she edits fewer student essays and isn't trying to host any more retreats). It's also hard to explain to other people what she does. But she doesn't want to stop and go back to working for someone else. So she told herself, *Who cares? It feels good to me.*

"I really got super grounded in like, *I'm just going to keep doing this*," she says.

At the end of the year, she realized she had paid the rent for a whole year. "I felt really proud," she says. "I haven't done that in a long time."

———

As she got closer to turning thirty-five, Sally started thinking about going back to Paris. It would be her first trip there since she'd been stranded four and a half years ago. She thinks about the city often, "but my body remembering that experience delayed any desire to go back," she says. She started to think it might be okay if she went, then started to actually want to.

"I still love it there," she says.

She began researching: *How much are flights? Where could I stay?*

She found a cheap flight for the week before her birthday, but she didn't book it. She needed a check from a client first. Last time, when she came back from Paris, she promised herself that before she went again, she'd have at least $7,000 in her checking account.

She also told herself she had to have a guaranteed place to stay the entire time. She reserved a no-frills hotel room she knew she could cancel.

When she got the check, she searched flights again. They were still cheap. She was going back to Paris.

Briefly she thought about asking Jay to go with her, but when she asked him what his work schedule was, he was going to be in the middle of shooting a movie during the time she had planned the trip. So she told him, "I'm going to Paris without you, just so you know."

"All right," he said.

"It would be nice to go with him at some point," Sally says. "But I don't think I'm super concerned about it."

In the weeks before she left, she started to feel nervous. She told some friends who knew what had happened during the last trip that she was returning, and they understood that it was a big deal. Some of them said they'd pray for her.

"You can pray for me, I guess," Sally says. "I don't know that it's making a difference, but it did feel nice that people would be thinking about me."

Her best friend told her, "It's going to be great."

As soon as she got off the plane and started to make her way through the airport and into the city, she started to feel better. *I know this place*, she thought. She knew the airport, the way to border control, and the escalator in a tube that would take her to the RER train to the city. When she started to walk to her hotel in the Montmartre neighborhood, she knew those streets too. She hurried past the few that were filled with men loitering and thought, *I know how to avoid these men*. Then she took a wrong turn, and for a minute she was anxious, but she figured out where she was and how to get to her hotel. As soon as she arrived, "that past trip was gone," she says. "The vestige of the previous time wasn't there."

She spent her days by herself, going on a lot of walks and eating a lot of baguettes. "I didn't see anyone there," she said. "I could have, but I was like, It's fine. I'm just going to walk around and relax and chill." She hesitated about going back to the Père Lachaise cemetery, where she'd spent the day bawling after she'd found herself with no place to stay on the last trip. But she'd been there every single time she'd been to Paris and, each time but the previous time, being there had made her appreciate her own life.

So one day she told herself to start walking and to keep going until she got there. On the way, she got a ham sandwich, some prosciutto, and her favorite dark chocolate Petit Écolier cookies, then found the spot she likes among the hills and grave markers, near her favorite sculpture of a chair that's tipped on its side. She ate her lunch and "it felt like I was coming back to center," she says.

CHAPTER THREE

Marrying

I'm hoping that as soon as my thirties are over,
I will look back and say, "Wow, I put it all on the
line and I'm glad I did."

—YASIN

There's a rhyme that was popular on the playground of my elementary school: *First comes love, then comes marriage.* As a kid, I was told that's how it's supposed to be.

For me, though, in my midthirties, it was more like I had a life full of love—not only men, but friends and work and living in a city that I still marveled at when I walked down the street—and marriage felt like a narrowing of that love. I was dating, and then I had a boyfriend and thought that eventually I would want a husband, but I was also having a hard time seeing marriage as a way to open up my life. I made a point of not centering my life around my boyfriend, hanging out with friends just as much as I did with him and being glad we had our own apartments.

For the first time, I was living by myself, and I loved closing the door of my apartment behind me and being in a space that was mine alone.

I saw marriage as it was presented to me in stereotypes: one spouse was always having to do what the other wanted, and I didn't want to give up my independence. And while society made the act of *getting* married seem important, actually being married was portrayed more like a drag: one spouse was bored with the other, or they were fighting over money or whose turn it was to take out the trash. I didn't know what marriage was like from the inside, or how to reimagine what I'd want mine to look like one day. All I could see was my fear that it would overshadow all the other things I was. I'd talk about marriage with my boyfriend, but it felt like we were talking about it because we were in our midthirties, not because we actually wanted to get married.

Friendships were something I could figure out on my own and construct how I wanted, and they became a huge part of my life, particularly with women. I felt like my friends and I had room to build relationships that were unique to us. This was especially true with Ruthie, who I met when we worked together at *Details.* We had a regular rotation of restaurants we went to for dinner. We walked together to wind down after work. During football season, we watched games on Sundays. In the summer, we went to the beach. She invited me to plays. I invited her to concerts. She cooked for me. I bought her fancy sneakers. She knew she never had to tidy her apartment before I came over, and I knew I could always show up in sweats. She stopped me from being too critical of myself. I told her to talk to me about anything. We have our own habits, traditions, and way of running our relationship, just like any pair of people who have been in each other's lives for a long time and know that they want to continue doing so, for better or worse. Whenever anyone asks me, "How's Ruthie?" I am always pleased because of what's implicit in the question: they know I will know.

In general my good friends are a support system—always there to talk out what any one of us needs. These relationships are sanctioned by nothing more than our love for each other, but they are as important as any other bonds in our lives. I never wanted a single tie to a romantic partner to overtake them, simply because it could be legally recognized. I also didn't want to pull back on the fulfillment I found in work and the freedom of organizing my life however I fancied.

But as time went on, I started to feel more solid in who I was and what I was doing and less afraid that marriage would take that away. I wanted to try a romantic partnership that went beyond deciding on joint weekend plans. My future spouse and I could shape our lives together.

So I asked my boyfriend to move in with me, a big step for a relationship that was built on no real commitment beyond seeing each other regularly and returning one another's texts promptly. I ignored how apprehensive I felt, which is easier to do when there are plenty of people who are telling you how good it is that you're taking steps to grow your life like you're supposed to. I thought eventually I would feel okay.

But as soon as he walked in the door of my apartment with a

bag on his shoulder, I knew I didn't want him there. I wasn't aware enough that I had made a mistake to form the words to say it right then, but I still knew on the hazy level before hard thought: *This isn't right.* What I should have done was break up with him immediately, but I was scared and felt like I'd already made too much happen to undo it in an instant.

The relationship took me a long time to end. During that time, I kept whipsawing between feeling that this was wrong and countering that maybe I just didn't understand what cohabitation was supposed to feel like. Then one afternoon, my boyfriend and I went to meet another couple, and as I watched them walk toward us, it was clear how united they were, even in such an ordinary moment and movement as them hurrying side by side to where we were waiting. I knew I didn't have what they did, and the revelation made me want to jump out of my skin.

———

Recently Sally and Jay had a fight. He was panicked about the future of their relationship. At thirty-three, he's two years younger than she is but thought by his early thirties he'd be married with kids. That won't happen by his early thirties anymore, but he told Sally, "I still expect to do that."

Unlike Sally, he's close to his parents. "He's, like, obsessed with them," she says. This is the first Thanksgiving he isn't going back to Detroit, where he grew up and his parents still live. He can't afford the plane ticket and is devastated he won't be there. If Sally celebrates holidays at all, she does it with her sisters. They usually have Christmas together, traveling to where one of them lives, what they call their "Sister Trip," and spending the day eating mac and cheese and apple pie, watching movies, and drinking wine.

Sally asked Jay what he wanted to do for Thanksgiving now that they were going to stay in Los Angeles, but he was so upset he wasn't returning to Detroit that "he doesn't even want to talk about it," she says, "and I'm like, *what?*"

He *did* want to talk about if he and Sally were going to get married and have kids, but Sally didn't think they needed to be so prescriptive. With smaller things, Sally still likes to plan and be organized. She has elaborate systems in place for how she takes care of her curly hair and tracks the novels she reads each year. But she tries not to be as heavy-handed with the bigger arcs of her life. She believes things will happen when they're meant to, if they're meant to. "I'm a spiritual person," she says. "I'm a person who thinks shit's going to work out. Something's going to happen. And he's not a spiritual person. He's not a believer in that."

Jay pressed her. "Do you even want to have kids?"

She could hear her mom in her head telling her that she's already too old to have kids. "I guess now I would have a geriatric pregnancy or whatever they're called when you're too old or your eggs are old or whatever," she says.

But she was resistant to saying that she definitely did want to have kids and agreeing to a time line. "I'm not opposed to the idea of having kids," she says, "but it's never been a thing where I'm like, 'And one day when I have a kid, I'm going to do this.' It was never a burning desire."

They ended the argument where they started, with Jay saying he wanted to get married and have kids and Sally saying she didn't care if they did or not. "I know being in the relationship feels good to me," she says. "I know that it helps me grow, and for that reason, I keep being open to it, but not because I think, *Then I'll get married, and then I'll have the three kids.* Maybe it will happen, and maybe it won't. I'm happy either way."

———

Today about half of US adults are married, a dramatically different share of the population than in 1960, when 72 percent of adults were married. The decline is due to a lot of changing behaviors. We're marrying later. The average age of first marriage for both sexes is older than it has ever been, and, we're cohabiting instead of getting married. More than half of people ages eighteen to forty-four have cohabited with a partner, a number that's risen steadily over the past two decades, according to the Pew Research Center.

In general, we aren't prioritizing finding a spouse or, in many cases, interested in having one at all. More than half of Americans ages eighteen to thirty-four surveyed by the Census in 2017 said that marriage is "not very important" to becoming an adult.

Why the apathy about the institution? Experts point to soci-etal shifts that mostly revolve around changing gender dynamics. Women no longer feel that we have to marry to have sex and be supported financially. Instead, we are using birth control and act-ing as our own breadwinners.

This isn't to say that women don't want to marry at all. I do, and I think so do many other women, but it's no longer the begin-ning of a life well lived. Our days are built around so much besides romantic unions.

In 1960, when Dorrie Jacobson was twenty-five, she was re-cruited to be a cocktail waitress at the Playboy Club in Chicago, the first one in the country. She'd been an aspiring actress in Philadelphia, performing in a play called *A Hole in the Head*, where she was playing a character who wore skimpy clothes and wasn't very smart. She made her entrance in a bikini, but when she got to center stage, the top fell off. The male star of the show crossed the stage, took off his jacket, draped it over her shoulders, and "we didn't miss a line," she says.

Afterward a Playboy representative came to see her back-stage. "I'm very impressed by your stage presence," he told her. "Would you be interested in being a Playboy bunny?"

She was. At the club, she loved wearing her uniform of a puffy tail and "a bit of cleavage" while serving drinks to a clientele of mostly celebrities and gangsters. To her mother's generation, and even most of her peers, what she was doing "was just about the same as being a prostitute," she says. But the admiration from the customers gave her confidence, and she was making what she describes as an obscene amount of money for the time, between $500 and $600 a week. She didn't need a husband to support her.

But at twenty four, she was already an old Playboy bunny—most of the other cocktail waitresses were in their late teens and early twenties—so as she neared her thirtieth birthday, her family and what seemed like the whole of society was telling her time was running out. Most women were married at eighteen or nineteen years old. "In your midtwenties you were the old maid," Dorrie says.

The message was: *What are you doing? You're almost thirty years old. You've got to settle down and do the things you're supposed to do.*

So she quit the Playboy Club and got married. "That was it," she says. "We all followed the rules in those days."

On her thirtieth birthday, she didn't have a party. "It was not something to celebrate at all," she says. "Instead, you went into a dark room, sat in the corner, and brooded. When you got to be thirty, it was, *It's all over now.* It was the turning point, which is absolute insanity when you think about it today."

The man she married was a good provider. He was in real estate and owned several apartment buildings in Philadelphia. But "it was a loveless marriage on my part," Dorrie says. She doesn't regret the daughter she had with him after they married, also following the rules, or that her daughter's birth was followed shortly thereafter "by a liberating divorce," she says. "I learned that you can't listen to anyone else telling you what to do. You've got to know yourself and what it is you want and go after it."

———

Yasin met Melanie on New Year's Eve. A friend dragged him to a party; he told Yasin he worked too much and needed a night off. Melanie's friend brought her for the same reason. Yasin started talking to Melanie. He doesn't spend much time on surface pleasantries. He's always probing to learn more about people. He asked Melanie about her work but wanted to know more than just what she did. He asked, "What are the parts of your job you're most passionate about?"

He thought that he wanted to marry and have children someday, "but I wasn't looking for anything at the moment because I was way too busy," he says. Melanie also wanted to marry and have kids, but worked as hard as he did and was starting her own company too. They began dating, and on these dates, often evaluated each other's evolving business plans.

After they'd been dating for about six months, they were walking around a farmers market in downtown New York. Yasin was uncomfortable. He needed to tell Melanie something but didn't know how. Already his parents had been asking him when he and Melanie were getting married, and when they'd be getting a grandchild. He *did* think he wanted to marry Melanie, but didn't know when, and realized that Melanie might be wondering the same things as his parents. He couldn't give her any answers either.

At the farmers market, Melanie could tell something was

bugging Yasin. They kept walking, with him getting increasingly somber, until finally, she stopped and asked what was wrong.

"We have to break up," Yasin said. It was unfair for him to keep dating her. He didn't have a stable income and wasn't sure when he would. Nor did he know when he'd feel comfortable getting married or having kids. He wasn't going to force her to wait for him.

Melanie listened, then said, "I reject your breakup. You don't have to protect me. I know what's going on. I know what I signed up for."

After the conversation, Yasin realized that she just wanted to be with him. She didn't need his career to be rock-solid, or exact dates for when they would marry and have children. "She wasn't waiting for perfection, and I didn't have to either," he says. "Things were good enough."

———

Sally and Jay haven't talked about marriage again. He was shooting a movie, she was traveling a lot, and now he's editing the movie, and she's been busy with the business she runs with her sister.

Jay brought up their relationship again briefly when he mentioned a friend who was separating from his wife. The friend told Jay he felt like he was living with his best friend, not the woman he fell in love with. "I don't want us to feel like we're best friends living together," Jay told Sally. "We should do things that make it so we don't feel that way."

"Okay, sure," Sally said, "although relationships are just friends who live together."

They used to hike a lot, or go on short, random road trips, but Jay sold his car, and Sally doesn't know how to drive, so they mostly hang out in their one-bedroom apartment. If they are actively wanting to spend time together, they'll be on the couch or in the bed, watching TV or a movie. Otherwise Sally will be working at her makeshift office at the dining room table and Jay will be in the bedroom trying not to disturb her. "It's a small apartment, so there's not a lot of places to go," she says. They used to cook, but lately they've been ordering a lot.

"In my wildest dreams we'd either be living in a large home, or we would be living separately," Sally says. "That's something I've been thinking about a lot. I really love having my home be a particular way, and that is not the way Jay likes his home to be."

Sally folds her clean laundry immediately and throws out any food she suspects is close to spoiling. Jay piles his clean clothes on a chair in their bedroom and leaves Styrofoam containers in the fridge for ages. "We don't even sleep the same way," Sally says. She's always hot. He's always cold. He needs the white noise machine on. She doesn't. Anytime he goes out of town, "the first thing I do is strip the bed and put on my sheets and my blanket," she says. "It's the Sally blanket."

She told Jay about her fantasy of them having separate homes one day. "I don't know about that," he said, "but oh, okay, that's cool."

"It sounds perfect," Sally replied.

———

Jill Filipovic, the author of *The H-Spot: The Feminist Pursuit of Happiness*, has written about how some women no longer see marriage as a way to kick off their adulthood. "We think about marriage and children as things we do once more of our ducks are in a row," she says, "once we've graduated from college, or grad school, depending, once we feel like we're financially independent from our parents, perhaps once we feel like we have enough money to buy a home. Once those things are in order, then it seems like we feel like, *Okay, now marriage might be the thing to do*, which is quite different from how it used to be. Marriage was kind of the first step to those other achievements."

I think men have shifted here too. They are also waiting to be secure in other areas of their lives before getting married—and for men, changing gender roles also means marriage will consume more of their time and emotions than when being a husband meant only being a provider. Aaron Weeks, a restaurant owner in Brooklyn, is cohabitating with a girlfriend for the first time at age thirty-nine, despite having a couple of long-term relationships in his twenties and thirties, in part because he was mindful of the responsibilities that come with living with a romantic partner. His parents have been married for forty-seven years and both of them, but especially his mom, made a point of teaching him that relationships are partnerships, financially, and also concerning domestic and emotional duties.

"I definitely had some reservation and anxiety," he says. "I was aware, not necessarily firsthand, that it's a lot of work. It's a totally different lifestyle. There's another level of responsibility to a person when you're cohabitating."

But men were never supposed to be as rooted in their families and homes as women. For women, delaying marriage—or opting out altogether—is such a significant broadening of how we move around the world, especially if we don't marry before what's called the "Age Thirty Deadline." Psychologist Meg Jay writes about this deadline in her book *The Defining Decade: Why Your Twenties Matter—And How to Make the Most of Them.* "The challenge I hear about most in my practice is related to what has been termed the Age Thirty Deadline," she wrote. "The Age Thirty Deadline is the quiet but nagging concern that so many twenty-somethings have. What to do about relationships in our twenties may not be clear—or even seem imminently important—but 'I'd better not be alone at thirty' is a common refrain."

She continued, "In my experience, the Age Thirty Deadline is more of an Age Thirty Bait and Switch. Everything that was okay at twenty-nine suddenly feels awful and, in an instant, we feel behind. Almost overnight, commitment changes from being something for later to being something for yesterday. Marriage goes from something we'll worry about at thirty to being something we want at thirty. When, then, is the time to really *think* about partnership? This sudden shift can lead to all kinds of trouble."

Jay's point in her book is that we need to spend our twenties treating every relationship as if it's supposed to lead to a lifetime partnership, "about *not* waiting to get picky until you are in your thirties and the save-the-dates start pouring in," she writes.

But I think she's wrong and is, in fact, perpetuating the same scare tactic that women have been subjected to for decades. *You're running out of time. It's now or never. Marry him.*

And, after you do, you'll have crossed some kind of finish line, and everything will be fine.

Katie Sturino, the founder of the beauty brand Megababe who got married when she was thirty-one, says she felt this pressure. "I was feeling, like, old, which is so funny," she says. "I was like, 'Oh man, I've been with this guy for ten years, and I really hope we get married because otherwise I've wasted my time.'"

After the wedding, she felt relieved and superior to those who weren't married. The feedback she got from other married friends and family was that she should have been. "Married people want you to be married, so they feel normal," she says. "It's like a club. It's a safety net. It's this feeling of *You're safe, you're like us.* We all made this choice. Not getting married is the less safe choice."

Two years later, her husband asked her for a divorce, which— after a year of her "being a maniac," she says—made her realize that the safety net of the marriage was an illusion. The social construct was just that and didn't mean anything unless both of them were going to keep being committed to each other day after day.

"He married me, and he still dumped me for someone who was twenty-four," she says. "That can happen whether you get married or not, whether you have kids or not, whether you anything."

Filipovic herself got married at thirty-four, almost a decade after she'd finished law school.

"Everybody craves meaning in their lives, something that makes them want to get out of bed in the morning," she says, "and for women traditionally, we were told that purpose was supposed to come from getting married and having babies and taking care of a husband and a home. And for a lot of women that didn't really fit the bill, and I think there are a lot of us now, myself included, who don't feel like that will give us much purpose, and in fact find that sense of purpose elsewhere. So I think that ability to seek out purpose in a wider arena is part of what is driving this kind of shift in adulthood."

To be sure, it's a privileged position not everyone is in. Not every woman can support herself, and some women want to be married but can't find the kind of partner they're looking for: one with a similar education level and professional prospects. Black women marry, on average, later than women of all other major racial and ethnic groups. Social scientists haven't been able to fully account for this difference, but empirical research points to labor-market disparities and other structural disadvantages Black people face, especially Black men. "My single friends and I can attest to the trials that come with having fewer dating options and outnumbering Black men in our college and professional lives," Angela Stanley, then a researcher at the Kirwan Institute for the

Study of Race and Ethnicity at Ohio State University, wrote in an essay titled "Black, Female and Single."

No matter what, the societal dictate still tends to be that women should be married (and have children). No less an expert on being pummeled with the constant supposition that she isn't happy because she's single and child-free, Jennifer Aniston told *Elle*, "We live in a society that messages women: By this age, you should be married; by this age, you should have children. That's a fairy tale. That's the mold we're slowly trying to break out of."

She continued, "Why do we want a happy ending? How about just a happy existence? A happy process? We're all in process constantly."

———

After my breakup with the boyfriend I lived with, I started thinking about an ex-boyfriend. The fact that I missed him made sense. We dated for a long time when we were in our twenties, in a period that made us both better, and I felt so many ways about him: he was delightful, charming, magnetic, gorgeous, but also infuriating and crazy-making. He was comfortable one minute, unpredictable the next, and had a million other traits that made me both unable to get enough of him and terrified that his big personality might dominate mine.

Even though we weren't in a romantic relationship, we had

remained close, texting and visiting each other when we could. We had mutual friends we hung out with too. It was a complicated friendship, and one where I often cringed at how opinionated he was and how unwilling he was to try to make nice with everyone. But, just as often, it felt easy—I liked doing everything with him, even once marveling how much I enjoyed a trip we took to the store to stock the Airbnb I was staying at with toilet paper and laundry detergent. He let me use his Amazon Prime account; he encouraged me to set up an LLC for my freelance business. I called him when my pet fish died. He called me the morning he thought he was going to get laid off. Once when we were biking with another friend to the beach in LA, I watched him in front of me, carrying his surfboard under his arm as he pedaled, and felt sure I should put aside the fear I had about being with him and go for it.

As scared as I was, I also knew that he was a person who challenged me. He supported that I wanted to stretch myself and let me have space to be intense and restless, and liked that I wondered constantly, *What's next?*

I didn't know that I could trust what I was feeling, and part of me was sure I needed to go sit in a corner by myself for a while, but what overrode that was a certainty that I was being pulled under by fear.

I couldn't sleep. I wanted to go talk to him in person, which after a string of no-sleep nights, turned into a more high-concept plan: I would get on a plane, show up at his doorstep, and ask him to marry me. At least part of me knew this was nuts, like a monkey drunk on rom-coms was in charge of my brain.

But it also felt urgent, as if this were my only shot to do this. It took me a day to buy a plane ticket. I kept hovering over the button that would make my purchase final. I booked a hotel too, knowing that there was a good chance I wouldn't be sleeping at his apartment after I proposed.

I also knew it was a selfish gesture. He wasn't expecting this. *Turn back*, I thought at the airport where I was waiting to transfer planes. *What are you doing?*

It was a Tuesday. I was sitting on the ground at the gate in ripped jeans. I had a dress in my bag that I thought I would change into, but as I waited to board, the reality of what I was embarking on stopped me from making this quest into even more of a spectacle.

On the plane, I Gchatted Ruthie, who knew where I was going: "This is such a mess."

At the time, she was an editor at *Oprah* and was in the middle of working on a story that was supposed to help people figure out what they really wanted.

"Stand by for some real Oprah shit," she wrote. "Soul Directions—whether conscious or unconscious, usually come in the forms of feelings, knowings, blurts, or flashes of insight. Like a small child who tugs."

She continued, "So I kind of think that happened to you, and I know it doesn't feel as certain now."

She kept typing me through the flight. Eventually, we decided

I should get off the internet and watch a movie to distract myself, but first she wrote, "I think you realized something about what you wanted and you should honor that."

We told each other we loved each other, and she said to call if I panicked when I landed.

Instead, when I landed, I went to his apartment building. In his lobby, I told the concierge who I was waiting for and sat there for long enough that I was sure I should bolt. *This is crazy,* I told myself. *Get out of here. Go to your hotel.*

"There he is," the concierge said, and I looked up to see him walking in the building, coming home from work.

I remember him being both confused and glad to see me. He kissed the top of my head. He repeated, "What are you doing here?" He told me he'd just booked a plane ticket to meet up with me and some other friends in a few weeks, as a surprise. We took the elevator to his apartment, and I did a nervous version of the speech I'd practiced on the plane. I said I wanted to marry him, and he took it all in thoughtfully. We talked, and I understood he loved me, but that he was dating someone else and really wasn't expecting me to show up. He was planning to buy her a Christmas present that night. We were broken up.

We talked a lot more, and I kept waiting. In retrospect, I guess I was waiting for him to say yes, but it was also nice just being in his living room talking to him, and we kept doing this for hours, until he finally said what surprise and care for me prevented him from recognizing immediately: "I can't give you a yes."

It was near midnight. He said he'd drive me to my hotel, and we were both crying as I put on my boots to leave. I'd figured out what I wanted, but it didn't mean that at that point in his life, he wanted it too.

———

Charles met his boyfriend, Matt, at a Jacksonville Jaguars football game. They were with different groups of friends, but some of those friends knew each other. Matt moved to introduce himself to Charles, and "I knew from that moment when I saw him walking over to me that I wanted to marry him," Charles says. "It sounds cheesy saying it, but I can still remember that moment to this day."

Marriage is important to Charles. He wants what his parents have. They've been together for thirty-eight years, although they divorced for a year early in their marriage before Charles was born and split again for a short period when he was ten. After he's married, he envisions "going on that nice honeymoon that everyone talks about, having two or three kids, going on a vacation once a year as a family, and continuing to grow in my job," he says.

Three years ago, Charles proposed to Matt. They were going to see pop singer-songwriter Ben Rector in concert. Before the show, Charles emailed Rector's management to see if he could propose onstage. He wrote: "Like any relationship, we have our fights, but we always come back to each other. I would do anything for him. As you say in 'White Dress,' 'I never knew that I could love someone the way that I love you.' He says I saved him, but in reality, he is the one that saved me."

Rector's management wrote back to say the band didn't allow onstage proposals, but: "We hope you are able to find a magical way to propose to Matt, as we are sure you will be!"

So Charles ended up doing it in the hotel room after the show. Matt started crying as soon as Charles knelt in front of him, before he could even ask, "Will you marry me?" But Matt wasn't ready. "Not yet," he answered.

Charles is frustrated that Matt wasn't ready to get married when he was—and hurt enough to declare that he won't be asking him again. If Matt wants to marry him, he's going to have to be the one proposing. "I've already done my job," Charles says.

But recently he hasn't felt close to Matt. They've both been overwhelmed by their jobs and schoolwork, and their relationship has started to feel like an obligation. For months, they've either been ignoring each other or arguing about money. They spend most evenings apart. Matt goes out with friends while Charles works. When they do go out together, other guys often flirt with Matt, "the most beautiful man on this planet," Charles says. Matt ignores them, but it still makes Charles mad and "then I act like an asshole for the rest of the night," he says.

They've been this way before. It leads to a big fight, makeup sex, and then, "you get back to where you were," Charles says. Matt hasn't gotten any closer to wanting to get married, hesitation Charles thinks is due at least in part to the fact that when he was a teenager his mom sent him to Exodus, a now-shuttered camp in Orlando, Florida, that instructed attendees they could choose to not be gay. The pastor at his mom's church suggested it. Because of what Matt heard at Exodus, he's hesitant to show Charles affection in public. He won't hold hands or kiss him when they're out, even though Charles wants that. "That also affects how he feels about getting married," he says.

Some days he tells Charles, "I want to get married and have a wedding."

Then he changes his mind, "because that means he will have to get married in public," Charles says.

Charles is open-minded and doesn't like to make harsh judgments about other people. With Matt, he wants to respect his reticence about getting married, even though Charles wishes they would do it now. He hopes Matt will be ready someday, but knows there's a chance he might never be. "The right thing with anyone is what's right for them at that moment," Charles says. "If a straight couple, they don't want to get married, they want to have ten kids, cool, then do it. There's a lot of stuff going on, and that's life. We do the best we can."

Matt and his mom are close today—and Charles is very much a part of their family too. She lives a forty-five-minute drive away in Middleburg, Florida, and on Thanksgiving, they spend most of the day with her, playing board games and watching TV, before they go to see Charles's family. Matt doesn't talk about his feelings much and has asked his mom only once why she sent him to Exodus. She said, "I was told that it was the best thing for you."

"I can halfway forgive people for it," Charles says, "because they grew up one way. You don't know what to do or how to handle it. To a point, it's maybe they didn't understand all the stuff they were doing at those camps."

When he was a teenager, Charles struggled with accepting that he was gay. At twelve or thirteen, he talked to guys in AOL chat rooms and printed out naked pictures of guys that he kept under his mattress. One day his mom, who had clearly seen what he was up to, asked him if he was gay.

"I can remember it, like an out-of-body experience almost, so very clearly to this day," Charles says. She was sitting in her home office. He was standing in the doorway, crying, denying it.

His mom said, "It's okay if you are. Just tell me."

"I kept denying it," Charles says. "In hindsight, I really wish I was okay with it enough to come out to her, but moreover to come out to myself at that time. It would have saved me so much pain and heartache."

A few years later, Charles found himself kneeling on his bedroom floor reeling about his sexuality and "crying and praying to God to make me 'normal,'" he says. "I did not want to be gay anymore. I did not want to have to deal with this anymore." He put the twelve-gauge shotgun his granddad had given him in his mouth, loaded. What kept him from pulling the trigger was thinking about his mom. "Nothing else," he says. "I just didn't want to hurt my mom."

When he was twenty-one, he was ready to tell his parents he was gay. He invited his mom to lunch and showed up with his boyfriend at the time. "Mom, I want you to meet my boyfriend," he told her.

"As always, my mom was such a doll about it all," he says.

To tell his dad, he wrote him a letter from boot camp. They never talked about what he'd written, but when Charles came home from boot camp, his dad jumped on him and hugged him, "like a spider monkey, legs and arms around me," he says.

———

I flew from my failed proposal back to my childhood home in Texas and confessed to my mom what I'd done. I was devastated my ex didn't want to be with me. I also thought, in the dark aftermath of all of this, that I'd never get married.

At the time, not being married seemed like an overwhelming loss, one that took away from all that I was happy with in the other aspects of my life. I remember telling my mom that I had nothing, which in the moment felt indisputable, as if all I'd ever wanted was gone because I hadn't gotten engaged.

It will all work out, my mom reassured me as I cried in her arms, like I was five and it was story time. I'm sure my mom meant that I'd find my way to marriage eventually, but as I stayed in Texas longer than I'd planned because I was too crushed to go back to New York, I started to think about why I wanted to be married. (I also watched all of *Gilmore Girls* and texted Ruthie a billion times.)

The part of my brain that could still see straight knew that marriage hadn't been important to me for a big part of my life, and for it to suddenly seem like everything didn't make sense.

For sure, I still wanted to be with my ex. I hoped he'd change his mind. He'd texted, "I hope you arrived safely" when I got to Texas. I held on to the text as a promising sign.

But logically I knew I could have a romantic commitment to him, or someone else, without being legally married. I believe that your family is who you choose it to be. I never wanted to put a greater emphasis on people who were tied to me by blood or the law than on people who were tied to me by love. I also didn't think getting married would make me any more adult. So why did I care so much about marriage right now? Was it just because I was rejected?

I kept thinking and concluded that, of course, I was hurt partly because I don't like to not get what I want, and I did want to be with my ex. But I also wanted to get married.

I always want people to know how much they mean to me, and I like to feel that back. I say "I love you" to my friends all the time. I hug hard. I'm liberal with hearts on social media and pretty much everywhere else. I often write to someone with nothing more than a message about how great I think they are.

With marriage, I wanted to publicly proclaim that I had chosen a romantic partner. I wanted to commit out loud to this person, and have him do the same for me. Whenever I fantasized about the wedding I might have with my ex, I didn't think much about the dress or food or dancing, only the speech I wanted to make about what I love and value about him. Marriage offers a neat way of saying, *You mean this much to me.*

I still wanted to make that speech to my ex, but I was also starting to be able to see through my initial sweeping despair—I knew that I needed to go back to New York. The evening I arrived, my friend Matthew, who I've known since eighth grade, met me on the sidewalk in front of my apartment, with snacks. He didn't want me to be alone. Inside the apartment, Ruthie had left flowers and a card on my dining table. Matthew and I ordered Thai food, Ruthie came over later, and we talked and laughed and were serious about what had happened in all of our lives since we'd last seen one another. That night, being surrounded by my friends, being *supported* by them, made me understand that my heartbreak wasn't as final as it felt like. In the morning, I'd get up. In the morning, I'd keep going.

———

Charles tried to accept that Matt might not ever want to get married, but he wants them to be married, so he's going to push for it. He also said he wouldn't propose again, but now that some time has passed since his first proposal, he's less hurt that Matt said he wasn't ready and is thinking about asking again. It's July. He might propose in the fall, on a trip, maybe to London again. On September 1, they'll have been together eight years.

This time, he's trying to prepare Matt for the proposal. "He knows I want to do it pretty soonish," he says. "We'll see how it goes. If he says 'No' or 'Not yet' again, then he can find some-where else to sleep."

Earlier in the summer, they went to a wedding in the moun-tains near Canton, North Carolina. They bunked with their friends in a huge cabin, Matt officiated the ceremony, and after-ward, "we just drank and had good times," Charles said. He sug-gested to Matt that they do something like that if they get married.

"I don't want to have a ceremony," Matt said.

"But that's the whole point of getting married," Charles said. "If not, it's just signing paperwork."

Charles didn't press Matt any more on why he didn't want a ceremony, but he wishes he understood. He suspects it's because of Matt's time at Exodus, but he'd never ask him that directly. If he did, he worries that Matt might get so mad that he'd decide he doesn't want to be with Charles at all, much less marry him.

By the end of September, Charles has booked a December trip to Toronto for the two of them, where he plans to propose. When he talks about the impeding proposal, it's like he's psyching him-self up to go for it again. "Matt definitely has a hang-up about it, but I don't care," Charles says. "We're getting married, and we're going to have a ceremony."

In the meantime, for their anniversary, they went to dinner at a Mexican restaurant. Charles was hoping for something more candlelit—"I like that movie-type romance stuff," he says—but he knows that's not really Matt. "So I just have to find that good compromise." For a few days as part of the Toronto trip, they're staying in a treehouse in the wilderness. That's where he's planning to ask Matt to marry him. "He's not going to say no," Charles says. "It's time."

———

Recently, Sally went on a road trip to Oakland with one of her best friends, who asked Sally if she cared about getting married. "I keep coming back to no," Sally says. "I don't give a fuck. If Jay decides it's important to him, maybe, but if he doesn't bring it up, I'm not going to bring it up."

In a few weeks, they're going to Jay's best friend's wedding. Sally avoids weddings when she can. Previously Jay had a friend get married in Detroit, and Sally told him she couldn't go because she had to work. "I could have gotten out of it," she says, "but I was also looking for an excuse. I just don't know that I care enough about weddings. They're so full of things I don't like." She often knows only one other person, or no one. The food usually isn't good. She doesn't want to get dressed up. "I have to wear heels or some shoe that's not a loafer, and it's just for a wedding," she says. "I'm excited you're getting married and that means something to you, but I don't care that much."

She's not likely to imagine what her own wedding might look like when she's at other people's either. "It's so removed," she says. "What other people do have nothing to do with me. It's like, *Oh, nice, whatever.* It's not like I'm a troll. I'm happy for them, but it's more of a detached feeling."

The wedding she envisioned having with her former fiancé was a picnic in the park. "I wanted to get fancy sandwiches and booze it up and hang out," she says.

This caused a fight.

"No, never," her former fiancé told her. "What are you talking about? I could never do that."

Along with deciding she doesn't care about getting married, Sally feels less and less like she wants children. "I've gone through various stages with both things," she says. When she first started dating Jay, he was very clear that he did want children, but since then, "I think he's opening up to other possibilities of not having to do things the way you're told you have to do them," she says. "It's within his journey that I've been able to come to the same conclusion as before. I don't care. I don't know that I would ever rule them out entirely, but when I evaluate where I am now and what things look like for the near future, I don't know that I want them."

The wedding Sally was dreading turned out to be one of the best weddings she's been to. Jay was in the wedding party, so, before the ceremony, he introduced her to two of his college friends. They befriended her immediately. As the guests were taking their seats, she was wandering, looking for a spot, and they stopped her.

"Girl, what are you doing?" they said. "Sit next to us."

The groom began sobbing as soon as he started walking down the aisle. "He was a fucking mess, and it was so sweet," Sally says. After dinner, they all danced and "a bunch of us did molly, so that was unexpected, but I was here for it," she says.

The night before, at the rehearsal dinner, she and Jay sat next to another couple who asked if they had kids. "If there are a lot of people of color, the chances of you having had children but not being married are very high," Sally says. "I don't think it comes up that way when I go to white people's weddings."

When they said they didn't have kids, the other couple asked if they were going to get married.

Jay answered for them. "We've talked about it," he said, "and I'm not opposed to it, but we're focused on the upward trajectory of our careers right now and neither of us is in a hurry."

While he was talking, he kept looking at Sally as if to ask, *Am I saying the right things?*

"It confirmed for me that he's not worried about it," Sally says. "It's good to get some confirmation because it was just in my head before that. It's one of those things where I said I'm not going to bring it up because I don't care enough. It would be weird to be like, *This is not at all important to me. Let's talk about it.*"

Charles bought Matt an engagement ring. It's a plain band made of hammered silver because "he doesn't like flashy," he says. When the package arrived, Charles put it on his nightstand and told himself not to open it. If he did, he feared Matt might peek inside the box. But he couldn't resist; he wanted to see the ring. "My stupid self got the better of me," he says.

He might not have been being stupid. Matt hates surprises. It's possible he wanted to warn him that he wasn't just talking about proposing—he had a ring. "Maybe subconsciously I knew he would look," Charles says. "Maybe I wanted him to."

Matt *did* look in the box, but Charles didn't find out he had until a few nights later when they got into a fight. They'd been at an all-day music festival in Jacksonville called PorchFest, drinking since 10:00 a.m., and they often fight when they're drunk.

They were at dinner with some friends, talking about work. Charles said something like, "Matt wouldn't be where he is if it wasn't for me." He didn't mean it the way it came out. Charles introduced Matt to the person who got him his first job in social work, and "I think it's cool that I introduced him to someone, and it turned into a career," he says. "You want to be part of your partner's life and you're proud. But when you're both drunk it's easy to misread intention."

Matt left the restaurant and walked back to their house, where their fight escalated into Matt telling Charles, "I know what's in the package, and I don't want it."

They repaired the damage the next day—both of them felt bad about the fight—but Matt didn't address what he said about not wanting the ring, and Charles was too scared to ask him if he really meant it.

The fight didn't change Charles's mind about proposing; he's still planning to do it in Toronto in December, even though he admits, "I'm doing a lot of assuming." If Matt really didn't want him to propose, Charles thinks, he would have broken up with him. "After the fight, he would have called it off and said, 'We're done,'" he says, but he didn't. "We made up and we're together."

He's been mulling how, exactly, he wants to propose. They'll get to the cabin in the wilderness, where he wants to do it, on the first night of their trip. But he thinks he will wait to ask until the next morning, while he's cooking breakfast. He's going to get on one knee again, but not immediately. "When you see someone in that position all brain thought stops," he says. "I want to say all the lovey-dovey, feel-good stuff and then get on one knee."

———

A year after Yasin tried to break up with Melanie at the farmers market, they married at their mosque. Melanie was Catholic when they met but converted to Islam. As she got to know Yasin, occasionally he would tell her about some facet of his personality, "I credit Islam with that." That made her curious about the religion. Without telling Yasin, she started to read about it and, eventually, decided she wanted to be Muslim too.

Yasin reveres Melanie. He talks about how skilled she is at running her marketing business and what a great mother she will be. He wouldn't have changed his mind about the marriage if she didn't convert. "The thing that mattered was if I liked her and if she was a good person," he says. But it was important to him that she be fine with raising their kids Muslim, which she is. "I would say that I lucked out," he says. "I don't think I deserved to have found someone so perfect for me, but I did."

They decided not to have a celebration after their wedding ceremony because they couldn't afford to replicate the only kind of reception they knew of, one held in a big event space with a sit-down dinner and a live band.

After about a year of marriage, though, they still wanted to have a party with their families and friends, so they decided to stop being hamstrung by the traditional way of doing it. They hosted a picnic at Liberty State Park in New Jersey, which overlooks the Statue of Liberty. It cost about $4,000, most of which went to the food, which was chicken and beef over rice from the Halal Guys food truck and baklava from a local bakery. "I still have white sauce in my fridge," Yasin says.

They've been talking about having kids, but Yasin doesn't want to start now, mainly because he doesn't think they make enough money to buy whatever a baby might need. "I don't know that we are as ready as anyone else to have kids," he says. But at the same time, he believes that at some point they're just going to go ahead and try. If Melanie gets pregnant, they will have to make it work. "We will put in the hustle," Yasin says. "I want to go one hundred percent with everything I do, that includes family, that includes business, that includes social life. I'm not going to have a chance to be thirty, thirty-one, thirty-two, thirty-three again. It's one year for each of those numbers, and I don't want to look back on it and think I wasted it. I want to think, *Wow, I went at it and I went at it hard and I'm glad I did*."

———

When Charles and Matt got to the rental cabin in the Toronto wilderness, the kitchen was smaller than it seemed in the pictures, with only an electric burner, and the fireplace didn't work. The plan Charles had for proposing was already screwed up. "All of the little things I had in my head, it was like that fell apart," he says.

In the morning, they decided to go out for breakfast instead of cooking. Charles carried the ring in his pocket, just in case. As they were driving the mile and a half to leave the 250-acre property, they stopped to take pictures of themselves on a snow-carpeted path lined with pine trees. Charles thought about proposing then. "It was a postcard, like how beautiful it was," he says. But after they took their pictures, Matt rushed back to the car.

Charles kept the ring in his pocket, waiting for an idyllic moment. In Toronto, they had dinner at the top of the CN Tower, which rotates above the city, and Charles thought about proposing at the end of the meal. But they started arguing a little bit, so he didn't do it then, or, eventually, on the trip at all.

"I was scared, or in my head," he says. "I didn't feel like it would have been that dream kind of thing that you see in the movies. I kept thinking, *I'll find a better time to do it*, but then another time comes, and then we're on the airplane back."

At home, he tried to figure out why he couldn't ask. He just wanted to get married. Why did his proposal have to be movie-perfect? "I've been a little childish in my thinking about it," he says, "trying to make it a fairy tale, like, *This is how you always see it happen, so this is how it should happen.* It has to be this super-cute romantic moment that you will regale everyone with until the end of time."

After thinking about it for a while, he realized that what he really wants isn't a flawless proposal. It's for Matt and him to be committed to each other as gay men, publicly and proudly. He wants to cast off everything he's done throughout his childhood and young adulthood to hide his sexuality and be Matt's husband. So a few weeks after they got home, a day or so after New Year's Eve, Charles resolved to stop trying to orchestrate the perfect proposal and just talk to Matt about wanting to marry him.

"I'm tired of carrying this around," he told him. "I'm tired of feeling like I'm scared. This is what I want, and I think that we should have this conversation openly and both be in agreement."

Matt said that he understood but that he wasn't ready to get married and that he didn't want Charles to ask him again. When he was ready, he would tell Charles—and then, he wanted to be the one to propose.

Charles agreed, even though he knows that letting Matt work through this on his own timeline means he won't be engaged soon. "I'm not expecting it to happen in the super-near future," he says.

Still, now he understands what he is really seeking and why. "I want to be able to wear a ring on my finger, just like everyone else," Charles says, "to celebrate all of the tough times that he and I went through, both as a couple and before we met, to say, *Yeah, we made it.*"

CHAPTER FOUR

Becoming Financially Independent

————

*There's often the sense that at some point you get to
where you are supposed to be and you take a deep
breath and stop for a minute. That hasn't come yet.*

—ADAM

When they moved to Los Angeles, Muriel was thirty-one and
Nick was thirty. They'd just gotten married and were going there
to attempt careers in comedy.

Nick noticed Muriel for the first time in eighth grade, but she
didn't notice him. She was busking, alongside her ten-year-old
brother, at a Seattle street fair called Folklife, singing show tunes
while her brother tap-danced. They put out a hat and used the
tips they got to pay for dance lessons (and chocolate-covered ba-
nanas sold at the fair).

"My brother and I used to have these horrible fights about,
like, what dance move matched the song and which song was fast
enough," Muriel says. Nick was a juggler, but he'd been too shy to

perform on the street more than a handful of times. He envied Muriel's confidence.

He didn't see her again until their senior year of high school when Muriel and her brother transferred to his school. They were in the hallway, and he remembered them immediately. "You guys used to tap-dance, right?" he said.

They became friends. Nick would go to Muriel's plays, which were mostly Shakespeare. He saw her as Edgar in *King Lear*, dressed as a boy, fencing.

"She was so good that it just made everyone else look so bad," Nick says.

They started dating in college, but when they decided to transition from being friends to being a couple, Muriel had a talk with Nick. She didn't want to lose their friendship if their romantic relationship didn't work out, so she told him that she didn't want them to feel obligated to stay together, a forced commitment that might make them hate each other. Instead, she wanted them to work on their relationship every day, "to make sure it was as healthy as we could make it and we were as happy as we could be." Getting married seemed like the ultimate forced commitment.

As they went through their twenties, moving from Seattle to Chicago together, they'd check in about marriage: "Does it mean anything to you yet?" or, "Where are we at with this whole marriage idea?"

It wasn't until they were moving from Chicago to LA that Muriel wanted to get married. It no longer felt like an obligation;

it seemed like a way to emphasize how important the relation- ship was to her. She was starting to think about her life and "fundamentally, it was like, *What do I want?*" she says. "Basically, I was looking at my stuff at the time and just feeling like my part- nership is the most important thing to me right now, out of everything."

Nick was excited to get married too. For him, doing it sud- denly seemed special. "It felt romantic and meaningful and sexy to just be like, *You know what, let's just commit to this. Let's just do it,*" he says. "The idea of doing the whole legal thing, and really do- ing that and bringing our families together, and making that hap- pen, felt like a big change, like a good big change."

They were married in a park in Seattle near the beach that Muriel used to play in as a child, under the cover of a camping shelter. It was raining a little, and Muriel's mom started a fire. Muriel wanted the justice of the peace to concentrate the cere- mony on the commitment of marriage because she thinks it's silly when the focus is on how great the people are or how their love is a love that has never existed before. "The coolest part about getting married is the union," she says. "What you're doing is huge, and there's a lot of power in that."

By the end of the ceremony, Nick was sobbing. There's a pic- ture of his mom trying to hug him while he's leaning back cover- ing his eyes because he's crying so hard.

"Doing it surpassed any of my expectations about what I thought it would be," Muriel says. "It was way beyond ritual."

———

What Nick and Muriel do in comedy is hard to define. They have a lot of projects going at once. Muriel performs in an improv group; Nick does stand-up. They have a podcast. They write scripts together. They created a web series; they're always applying for creative grants and fellowships.

But they don't make much money from any of these projects and both still work restaurant jobs. Muriel is a waiter; Nick, a bartender. It's been five years since they moved to LA—they're thirty-five and thirty-six now—and Nick thought they'd have accomplished more, and that they wouldn't have to work in restaurants anymore. Before LA, they'd been in Chicago, living a more low-key version of this life: waiting tables and acting in the city's sketch-comedy scene. "We moved to LA because the entertainment industry is out here," Nick says. "There are a lot more job opportunities. It was a decision to get professional."

They live in a one-bedroom apartment in the Fairfax district and share a car, a 2008 Honda that Muriel's grandma gave them. Muriel doesn't drive. The restaurant she works at is close enough to walk to and, when she needs to go anywhere else, Nick tries to drive her. The car had only sixteen thousand miles on it when they got it, and now it has sixty thousand miles on it. Nick estimates it will last another two hundred thousand miles, so they have a little while, but "we have to make it before the car craps out," he says.

Other friends who were going after the same kinds of careers and haven't made it have either quit altogether or are now acting or writing only as a hobby. "There's very few of us who are still slugging it out and still haven't done it yet, and are still waiting tables and kind of feel like we're still at the starting line," he says. "I tend to feel some pretty decent shame about it. I have friends who are fully launched and are somewhere on the spectrum of just having cool careers to pretty damn famous. Like they're on TV and they're at the Emmys. I'm speaking specifically of people we started with in Chicago, not to mention a ton of people we maybe were parallel with for a while in LA, so definitely I feel embarrassed that I still have to wait tables."

When they first moved to LA, they couldn't even find jobs at restaurants. No one would hire them. Instead, Muriel saw a job posting for a stand-up comedian at a strip club and suggested Nick apply. For his interview, they bought him a Calvin Klein suit at Marshalls that she hemmed with tape and staples. He got the gig, which was to introduce each woman before she performed. He was paid $10 a woman, and forty to sixty women danced each night. "It sustained us for like two years," Muriel says.

Eventually, Muriel found a job waiting tables, but she was extremely depressed. They were in a new city, there to really try to establish careers in comedy, and nothing seemed to be happening. "It was a scary time, and I didn't know how to handle it," she says. "I couldn't even wait tables without crying." At the time Nick was doing tons of stand-up, which meant she spent a lot of nights alone.

"We were super separate," Muriel says. He'd go to his gigs, and she'd feel guilty for spending her free time doing nothing to build the career she wanted. She told herself she should be looking for auditions, writing, or working with her improv group, but instead she mostly lay on the floor and berated herself.

"I kept thinking that I'm like this garbage person who isn't goal-oriented," she says. "The American dream is a meritocracy. The people who make it are the people who earned it. If you haven't made it, you haven't earned it. If you haven't made it, it's easier to slip into this thing of, *I'm lesser than.* I was actively telling myself that I'm not good enough to be better, and I was so fucking sad all of the time."

Eventually Nick realized that if he wanted to make money as a stand-up he was going to have to do more than two gigs a week. He would have to hang out at comedy clubs, go to shows he wasn't booked at, and take road trips to clubs around the Southwest. But he didn't want to do those things, so he and Muriel started collaborating more, writing scripts and performing together, a level of intertwined-ness that varies depending on what they're working on.

The main fight they have is that Nick would be fine to keep doing what they're doing for the rest of his life. That doesn't mean he doesn't want to be able to leave their restaurants and work only in comedy, but even if they don't seem to be moving toward that, he's not going to want to give up. "I don't really believe in having any other kind of job for me personally," he says. "I can't really imagine deciding enough is enough. As much as I sometimes feel panic, sometimes shame, for the most part, my heart is still pretty happy."

Muriel likes their life too, but she wants to feel like she's moving forward—she fears they're stagnating. Working in restaurants, and getting the money that comes with that, might be making them too complacent. She can make enough money for a week from only two brunch shifts, leaving the rest of her time free for her and Nick's creative projects, which mostly don't pay.

"It eliminates the need for me to be hungry enough to find a good writing gig," she says. "I just want to make sure we're active. I never feel like, *I want to stop doing this life.* I like what we're doing, but I want to make sure it's not becoming rote. If you wanted to, it's easy to make a web series and paint in your living room and work at a restaurant. That life can be a life. I like to think of what I'm doing as building a foundation for a stronger life in the future."

At the same time as she wants to be constantly moving forward, she also wants to take a night off and not feel like she should be doing something productive instead of drinking wine and listening to the podcast *True Crime Brewery.* It's part of reckoning with the reality that even though she and Nick are working as hard as they can to get jobs they love, it may never happen. And if they're only looking to a future goal that they might not achieve, they may miss getting any enjoyment out of the present.

"Lately, I'm trying to allow myself to say, *You need a break,*" she says. "*Don't think you're being too indulgent.* A lot of people I know are like that, like we feel bad all of the time. A big part of our operating day-to-day is shaming ourselves into doing something we think we should be doing. I'm like my own worst enemy. I would never talk about someone else the way I talk about myself in my head."

———

In 2016, when Marissa Mayer was the CEO of Yahoo! she gave an interview where she said that working 130 hours a week was possible, "if you're strategic about when you sleep, when you shower, and how often you go to the bathroom." Her exact strategy for sidelining basic needs in service of work was mocked, but the concept that you should always be working really wasn't.

At the time, I was an editor at Yahoo! Style, Mayer was my boss (if you went up a bunch of levels), and working all the time was my reality.

My position was supposed to be temporary. I was filling in for a few months while they were short-staffed. As a contract worker, I didn't have benefits, but I did have a regular paycheck (unlike when I was relying only on freelance writing work). At Yahoo!, employees were expected to be available anytime, and I was.

I checked email and Slack on my phone as soon as I woke up, immediately after I got off the train on the way to work, and again on the way back. If I happened to have service on the subway and saw something I needed to respond to right away, I got off the train at whatever stop I was at to do it. I worked late most nights, but even so, I carried my company laptop home with me every night in case I needed it in the few hours before I went to sleep. The last thing I did before bed was check my email. I worked for a few hours every Saturday and Sunday.

When I was at Yahoo!, I was working all the time, but only on my own ascension, which is what I observed most of my peers doing too. I saw a straight path from hard work to solidifying the career I wanted, and until recently, didn't think about how privileged that belief was. Both the #MeToo and Black Lives Matter movements made me examine many aspects of what I was part of in the workplace, reckonings that, at the time, shocked me. I'd been working for fifteen years and thought I was conducting myself as well as I could be, but I wasn't.

Focusing only on my own work—and the success I got from doing this—allowed me to ignore the sexist and racist behavior I was both part of and heard about secondhand. When I learned about an editor being sexually harassed by a superior at a business lunch, I was uncomfortable. When the sexism was directed at me—a group of male editors a few seats away from where I was sitting mocked a story I'd written; a boss asked me if I ever cheated on my boyfriend—I was frustrated I wasn't being taken seriously. But I never said anything about any of this behavior— to anyone else on staff or to human resources—and my silence meant that I never saw my progress as a writer and editor significantly impeded. When a magazine I worked at ran a racist story about Asian Americans or when a Black intern was laughed at for his memo suggesting more Black celebrities be featured on the cover (and told that those issues don't sell), I didn't speak out either. I remember thinking that the people who gathered outside the office to protest the racist story, and the intern who wanted to see more Black cover stars, were right, but I did not join the protest or stand up for the intern. I didn't try to change the system I was working in because it was working well enough for me.

Connie Wang wrote in Refinery29 about what she called the "'Grateful to Be Here' Generation" who never called out the system in which we worked. Instead, "we were supposed to find ways to exist within the broken system, by heeding the unspoken rules, watching our own backs, and privately fixing things when they went wrong," she wrote.

Today many younger workers aren't doing that. They bring issues to human resources, and if they aren't heard there, to social media or the press, in an effort to get fair treatment for themselves and everyone in the workplace. Unlike what I was doing and what I believed, the work they're doing goes beyond trying to bolster their own careers. It's hard to look back and know that my silence helped the culture stay how it was. My complicity was part of the problem. But it gives me hope that I still have a lot of my career left to go: I can stop doing only what helps me, be aware of and speak out against racist, sexist, and unfair behavior, and make space for others to have the same opportunities I did.

But at Yahoo!, I was consumed with only my own career, both with my job there and the work I was doing outside of it. In addition to being available whenever the website needed me, I was writing articles for other publications and had started putting together a book proposal. I had freed myself from thinking that my career would lead me to figuring out the rest of my life, but I still believed that all this work would eventually result in enough security that I could stop working so much. I just didn't know when that would be. Would it be after my contract ended at

Yahoo!? Would it be after I sold my book? Would it be after my savings account reached a certain number?

I sensed that this place, where my career and finances were stable enough that I could relax, was somewhere in front of me. But I knew it wasn't that close, and when my boss at Yahoo! asked if I wanted to stay at the job longer, I said yes.

———

Nick and Muriel just started auditioning for commercials, something they hadn't done before. For years, friends have been telling Nick that all the time he's spent making blasé comedy crowds like him was perfect training for making blasé commercial directors like him. And that being in commercials could help them get noticed enough to land guest spots on television shows. Nick didn't listen.

"I was just like, *I'm going to do my own stuff,*" he says. He thought veering from his and Muriel's projects would mean they were giving up. But part of him also knew that it could be a good move and that he was scared to be judged at these auditions. What if he failed?

According to Nick, at least half the auditions go like this:

"What's your name?"

"Hi, I'm Nick."

"Are you willing to shave?"

"I am."

"Nick, tell me about a time you had a funny experience with a cat."

"And then it's like, 'Oh my God, I found this cat when I was five years old . . .'"

He's booked a few nonunion commercials, which pay less but are easier to break into, including the second one he auditioned for. It was for Las Vegas tourism, and all he had to do was act like he was doing stand-up. In the end, he didn't even make the final version of the commercial, but he still got paid. When he got the check, he thought, *I'm on the board.*

Muriel booked a commercial too, for the travel site Booking .com, where she played "a single lady looking at buffalo," she says, but she was less jazzed about her experience. It was cool to be on set and have her own hair person, but she had to take the day off waiting tables, and, since the commercial was nonunion, after paying for a Lyft home (Nick drove her there), agency fees, and taxes, she made less than half of what she would have if she'd waited tables for the day.

"When you tell people you were in a commercial, their expectation is that it's a blind sort of good thing," she says. "No one wants to be receptive to the reality of it. Obviously it's a good thing. Hundreds of people audition and don't get anything, but no one wants to have a frank conversation about it."

Muriel is mixed race: her dad is Black; her mom is white. She has corkscrew curls, crooked teeth, great skin, and a striking smile. Sometimes she looks white, sometimes what casting directors call "ethnically ambiguous." She feels good about her body but says, "I'm the heaviest person in the room because we're in LA." The commercial industry has been moving away from casting only blondes with perfect teeth, and now directors say they're looking for real people, but most of the time they don't hire Muriel. "I get called back all the time," she says. "I'm a good actor, but people have no idea what to do with me. I'm happy with how I look, but then they don't cast me. In a callback, it's about looks only."

Nick and Muriel have also been entering their web series into film festivals. The premise of the series is that Drake has an extremely dorky brother and sister he hides in Canada; he doesn't want the public to know about his siblings, but they are obsessed with him. Nick and Muriel wrote it together. Muriel plays Drake's sister, and Nick directed it. They filmed eight episodes in seven days, then Muriel taught herself to edit so they didn't have to pay anyone to do it. At first, they put the series on YouTube, but when it got only three hundred views, "we decided to go hard with the film festival stuff," Nick says, which they hope will get the series seen by people looking for projects or for talent to hire.

They both admit they applied to too many, spending $2,500 on applications, "maybe more," Nick says. "It was like I was drunk online shopping. I was just like, 'Ooh, Minnesota, what are the categories?'"

"There was like the BoneBat horror comedy festival," Muriel says. "It was like, 'What are we submitting to that for?'"

"We submitted to some dumb shit," Nick says.

Still, waking up, checking their email, and hearing from

another film festival they were accepted to "is like Christmas," Muriel says. They're still trying to figure out exactly how many they're going to but think they'll be involved with film festivals for the rest of the year.

At their first festival, the Pan African Film Festival, their episodes were screening at 8:00 p.m. Muriel had been nervous all day. By the time she was in the back of a completely full theater, she was sure she was going to throw up.

Both she and Nick have gotten laughs when they're onstage doing improv or stand-up, but they've never sat in an audience waiting for their reaction to something they created and feared was funny only to them.

"Muriel plays the dumbest character," Nick says. "If it failed, it would be a hard fail."

As their series began, Muriel got even more scared they were going to bomb. "It's all strangers," she says. "It starts and, like, we made it in such a vacuum."

But then, at the first joke, eight seconds in, people started laughing—and they didn't stop. "If that happens for you, if you're with strangers and they're laughing from the very first second that your funny idea is presented to the end, you're just like, *We fucking did it*," Nick says. "It feels so crazy good."

Afterward, audience members kept coming up to them to tell them how hilarious the series was. "They had tears in their eyes," Nick says. "People went crazy for Muriel. They loved her. They just lost their minds. It was exhilarating. It was the most rewarding creative night of my life."

———

Our culture tells us to hustle, to rise and grind, and that what we really should be doing is working (oddly, this doesn't square with the equally pervasive cultural mandate that self-care will save you).

Initially, tech firms brought about this always-on existence with smartphones, which allowed us to stay connected to work wherever we were, and perks, like free string cheese and seltzer, that encouraged us to spend more time at our desks. They also tried to convince employees that they were working to advance the company's high-minded mission, not just its IPO valuation. All of this bolstered the idea that life outside the office wasn't as important as life within it.

That thinking transcended the tech sector and became an overriding way to work. You don't have to be carrying a start-up-branded tote bag to feel like, as screenwriter and illustrator Jonny Sun wrote on Twitter recently, "The only difference between weekdays and weekends is that you have more time to get work done on weekends."

But what is all of this work for?

Most of us don't have the security that workers who came before us did. We don't have steadily rising salaries, jobs we're confident that we'll be at for decades, and pensions that will support us in retirement. And our financial situations are far worse than our parents' were at the same age. "We have far less saved, far less equity, far less stability, and far, *far* more student debt,"

Anne Helen Petersen wrote in a viral story for BuzzFeed about millennials feeling burnt out.

The coronavirus pandemic, and the skyrocketing unemployment that resulted from it, only made our economic prospects worse. In July 2020, more than a million people had filed for unemployment for nineteen consecutive weeks, but statistics show that older, white workers are more likely to find new jobs more quickly than younger people and minorities. Steven Rattner, a former Treasury official, said on MSNBC's *Morning Joe*, "There are enormous differences in the impact of this joblessness, and people with more education who are more in the middle of their careers and frankly who are white are faring a lot better than many of the rest of our American colleagues."

A large body of research shows that young adults are most harmed by recessions, and for those in their thirties who started their careers during the aftermath of the 2008 recession, the economic destruction caused by COVID-19 is another blow in barely a decade. An analysis by the McKinsey Global Institute noted that this age group is "now going through its second 'once-in-a-lifetime' downturn."

Workers in the United States used to be more supported, at least if those workers were white and male. After the end of World War II, manufacturing was flourishing, and unions were powerful. As a third of the workforce, they had a huge effect even on the nonunion sector. The government, business community, and labor agreed to protect workers, in return for workers working hard and consistently.

"Until about 1980 productivity and wages in the US were pretty well linked, so basically ordinary workers were getting a big chunk of the overall economic returns," says Jacob Hacker, a professor of political science at Yale University and the coauthor of *American Amnesia: How the War on Government Led Us to Forget What Made America Prosper.* During this time, the government was also creating social protections, like expanding Social Security and passing Medicare and Medicaid.

In the eighties, the unions became less powerful, due to the increasing globalization of the US economy and the government bolstering corporations, a charge that was led by President Ronald Reagan. He encouraged businesses to transform toward a financial model driven by the stock market, which benefited CEOs and shareholders, while at the same time declining to protect workers. The government also pulled back on tax money that might be used to develop new social protections, like paid family or sick leave, or universal health care.

What started in the 1980s led eventually to where we are today, where even as we work all the time our jobs are becoming worse, with lower pay, worse benefits, and less job security—a situation that has become all the more dismal during the coronavirus pandemic and the economic spiraling that followed. "We put up with companies treating us poorly because we don't see another option," Petersen writes. "We don't quit. We internalize that we're not striving hard enough."

During the crisis, the government did rush to provide some protections for workers that didn't exist before, such as more generous unemployment benefits and unemployment insurance for gig workers, but those changes, at least so far, aren't permanent. Whether this forces a long-term restructuring of social policy is uncertain. Hacker, who was born in the early 1970s, is optimistic it might and points out how few protections American workers have compared to workers in other countries, such as us not having paid leave, universal health care, or a more inclusive unemployment system. "I see more prospect of fundamental change because of the pandemic than at any point in my lifetime," he says. "It may have taken a pandemic to lay bare just how unequal and insecure American workers are."

———

At thirty-six, Adam is a stay-at-home dad in Grand Rapids, Michigan. He, his wife, and two daughters, who are five and three, moved there about a year ago. Adam was thirty-one when his oldest daughter was born. He quit his job as an English as a second language teacher to take care of her, then stayed at home when his second daughter was born. For most of his thirties he's been responsible for the kids all day while his wife works. This wasn't how he thought he'd be spending the decade, not that he doesn't enjoy it, but "when I kind of imagined how I would be living out my thirties, what I would be doing specifically, being a stay-at-home father never crossed my mind," he says.

But when his first daughter was born, his wife made more money than he did, and her job had health-insurance benefits, while his didn't. They looked at daycare options but decided that they were so expensive it made more sense for Adam to stop working and take care of their new child.

Adam writes fiction, something he started to do after reading the Lord of the Rings trilogy when he was eleven, so the new arrangement also gave him time to write. He wrote a novel but wasn't able to find an agent who wanted to sell it, so he wrote another one and has been seeking an agent for it.

"It does feel like I've been doing significant work on both the parental front and the creative front," he says, "but at the same time, I've also felt isolated and obscure. Being a stay-at-home dad with very young children is very isolating. You're just around kids all day, and you can only talk about what kind of Play-Doh you want to play with for so long, and then along with that, I've written two novels that no one wants to read thus far. I've been able to do important work, and work that's meaningful for me, but I've gotten very little compensation for that or recognition outside of my own family."

Adam and his wife went to a Christian college, Calvin University in Grand Rapids, where the culture was to find a spouse while you're there.

"You graduate on a Friday and get married on a Saturday," he says, "but the thought of getting married at twenty-two seemed ridiculous to me."

He felt too young and unsure of what he wanted in life to commit to marriage, so he spent a few years while he and his wife were dating trying out different experiences: He worked as a sales clerk in a bookstore in Grand Rapids. He moved to Chile, where he taught English to Chileans in Santiago and Valparaíso.

During this time, he didn't have any concerns about his masculinity. Adam is white and grew up in Warsaw, Indiana, a politically conservative town of about thirteen thousand people that's known as the center of the joint-replacement industry. Both national and global orthopedics companies are based there. For a summer, Adam worked at one, polishing joints on the overnight shift. As a kid, he didn't have much in common with the other guys in town. He was artsy and listened to indie rock that none of his friends were into, but that didn't bother him. In college, when he was around more people, he met friends who shared those interests. He voted Democrat, read feminist-theory books, and didn't think he should be any other way.

"I always told myself, not without cause, that I was not a typical male," he says. "I wasn't a jock. I wasn't going to grow up to work for my dad's insurance company. I'd always thought of myself as *not* whatever is meant by a typical American male. And to a certain degree I would say that's not wrong. But as soon as I started staying home with the kids, with my intention of being a stay-at-home dad, I started worrying that I didn't measure up. It was a very strange thing to feel that way because I never really wanted to measure myself against a typical American man, but now I was putting myself against that standard and failing to live up to it. And that's kind of where I started to realize, I had bought into more typical definitions of masculinity than I realized."

Adam is good at the job of being his kids' main caretaker,

probably better than his wife would be. He can keep his emotions even, rarely losing his temper. He can also withstand the solitude that comes from being stuck in the house with small children, and do the grunt work of making them sandwiches and getting them juice boxes without complaining. But on a level above his daily routine, he has doubts if this is what he's supposed to be doing as a man. "That feels like an ongoing thing that I haven't resolved in any way," he says. "It's not like it's the greatest struggle in the world, but it's just been a continual realization of, I think I have a lot more anxiety about being a man, about failing to be a man, than I suspected."

Much of this is wrapped up in the supposition that men are supposed to be the providers for their families. Adam is proud that he contributes to their family through his time, not his income, but sometimes when the reality of money and not having enough of it comes up, he questions his choice.

Before they moved to Grand Rapids, his family lived in Indianapolis and had just put a down payment on a two-bedroom house with a huge backyard when his wife's position at the retail chain she worked for was eliminated. They no longer had an income, and the bank took away their mortgage. After floundering for a few months, their family of four moved in with his in-laws.

"That's something I never expected to have happen," Adam says. "I was ashamed about it. It felt like we'd failed a test, and we had to end up doing that." Both Adam and his wife grew up in homes where their families didn't have much money for stretches, but "they didn't have to move in with family members," he says.

Adam realizes his parents had more stable jobs, and it's different these days. Enough of his friends have been laid off that it seems like a rite of passage, and wages aren't keeping up with the cost of living—and haven't been for a long time. "I know that's true," he says, "but that doesn't make me feel all that better. That knowledge didn't take away any of the shame of having to move in with my in-laws."

They lived with them for eight months, which "truly isn't that long, all things considered," he says, "but eight months with your in-laws while you have two young kids can feel like a long time. It felt like a new kind of life experience that we hadn't anticipated."

They moved out when his wife got the job in Grand Rapids, working for their college alma mater. They were able to buy a two-story, three-bedroom house there, with a $15,000 down payment from a combination of money that Adam had inherited from his grandfather and that his wife had saved from her temporary job while they were living with her family.

Today they own a home, and his wife has a full-time job, but their situation still feels precarious. They aren't trying to work their way up to the next rung on the economic ladder; they're trying not to fall off.

"It feels like we have just enough," Adam says. "If someone has to go to the emergency room, or if we have to buy a new car, our circumstances could be changed in such a way that we could be in dire straits financially. My wife likes her job, but there are days when she doesn't want to go in, which is a pretty normal way to feel about a job, but she's very aware of the fact she's supporting a family of four on her single income, and that responsibility definitely weighs on her."

What happens when you realize all this work won't result in what you dreamed it would?

I did sell the book proposal I had been working on and, in my midthirties, wrote my first book, about the power of female friendship. When I started writing it, I was still working at Yahoo!, and in my head I was constantly calculating how much I had to accomplish and how impossible it seemed that I would be able to. Each day, I'd tabulate the number of interviews I needed to do and the number of words I needed to write to finish the book by the deadline. Those numbers kept getting bigger as I failed to complete what I told myself I had to. And as I kept writing, I questioned if I really knew what I was doing: if my message was clear, if I was accurately representing the women I interviewed, if anyone would want to read the book when I was done. It was like I was chasing after a ball that kept picking up speed as it rolled away from me.

Eventually, I quit my Yahoo! job to finish the book. I had saved enough money to do it comfortably and liked the idea of concentrating on one thing. After the book came out, it resonated with readers, which I am still so grateful for. Other women told me I'd said exactly what they wanted to about their own friendships.

From this high, I wanted to write another book and thought this might be the resting spot I was looking for. I could write a new book, stop freelancing and doing fill-in jobs, and take a lot of deep breaths.

This did not happen. It took me a long time to hone what I wanted to write about, and the churning in my head, my bank account, and my self-confidence started again. I sold the proposal, but the new book couldn't be my only job.

To make enough money, I'd need to write it while doing any other work I could. And, what seemed even worse to me, if the new project didn't resonate with readers like my first one had, any progress I'd made would be gone. All of what I'd been working toward could vanish, and it would be like I'd never done anything at all.

In the midst of this, my coworking space closed. It was part of a start-up called Spacious that rented freelancers spots in restaurants that weren't open until dinner. We could work at booths or high-top tables until around 5:00 p.m., when the first diners arrived. I loved going to Spacious and being around other people who were trying to do their best without the protection of a big company or real office space. It felt like the ideal of a coworking space: we were working together even though we weren't.

WeWork, the coworking company known for its luxury office spaces for start-ups, bought Spacious just after announcing its own IPO. Then that IPO imploded.

It turned out that WeWork's business plan and profit projections were lies. Many of the people creating the careers and companies they dreamed of in its open-plan offices while drinking fruit-infused water weren't paying the kind of fees WeWork said they were. They couldn't afford to. After the IPO failed, the CEO walked away rich, but the employees didn't—twenty-four hundred of them were laid off.

WeWork shut down Spacious, and I went back to working from my bedroom and thought about the ideal of working as hard as you could to create the career you wanted, then enjoying that.

For many of us, that straight line is gone, no matter if you're working for yourself, a small company, or a large one. Our job security was shaky even before the coronavirus pandemic, but now reliable work is more unpredictable than ever. Instead, what's increasingly, depressingly, certain are layoffs, pay cuts, reduced hours, not enough work, and furloughs.

Within this instability, our ambition can feel pointless, "like misplaced energy, as helpful to achieving success as chronic anxiety," Maris Kreizman wrote in an essay on Medium a few months into the pandemic about feeling like she had nowhere to put her professional ambition when so many industries, and life as we knew it, felt so uncertain.

"Where does ambition go when jobs disappear and the things you've been striving for barely even exist anymore?" she wrote. "My personal ambition still roils in my belly, but the path forward is less clear than ever."

I feel the same way. I like what I do and feel lucky that I get to do it. When I'm writing, I'm pumped up and hopeful I'm creating something people will connect with. But even so I'm a little beaten down. I don't think I'll ever get to the place I once thought was available to me, where hard work propelled me to a kind of career calm. The churning isn't going to stop.

———

The restaurant Nick works at is closing. Right before the Fourth of July, he learned that he'd be out of a job in a month. He and Muriel knew this could happen—the owner seemed to be losing interest in running the place, and restaurants can shut down with no notice. But it still felt abrupt. Nick had to work on the Fourth, so he sent an email to everyone he knew saying: *Instead of a barbecue, come to "Nick's Losing His Job Fourth of July Party."* None of the cooks showed up that night, he and his friends ate chicken fingers and french fries, and "I told the world I was losing my job," he says. "It was sort of helpful."

He had another reason for bringing his friends together. He thought they might be able to help him find his next job. He and Muriel decided that he should try to get an entry-level position in a writers' room or at a production company, jobs he didn't want to go after when they first moved to LA because it would have meant working in an office instead of on his own comedy.

"There for sure is a concession there," he says. "I told jokes onstage. I put stuff on the internet. I did a podcast. I did a web series. I've been creating content and being funny in the world, and that wasn't enough to make me the next Lena Dunham."

He's been booking commercials, but they don't pay enough. Plus, it's been a few weeks since his last audition. And while they've been going to film festivals, they realized that they don't have enough connections to producers or directors, people with power to back their projects. Working in an office with them could change that.

The shift could be good, but that doesn't completely counteract Nick feeling as if he failed. He emailed a friend who got him a shot at being a writer on *Jimmy Kimmel Live!* a few years ago. He didn't get the job then. Now he was reaching back out, hoping for a lower-level job.

"It's like, *Hey, remember me, I'm even worse off now,*" Nick says. "It's a tricky place to be in. I'm basically Aziz Ansari years old. I'm Hannibal Buress years old. I'm surrounded by people who are like me and are wildly successful, and that's not my story or path at all. I'm thirty-five and being like, *Shit, I guess I'll go be an assistant.* People are trying to talk me out of feeling bad about being old. A lot of people are saying I'm being histrionic. When I see who's an assistant, I know that it's fine for me to be one too, but it's just a chip on my shoulder."

Muriel wants to let Nick be bummed about his career not going like he envisioned but also thinks he has to forget about that fantasy. "I think it's been kind of a long time coming," she says. "We have pretty different personalities when it comes to that stuff. I know it's sad, and he should have the space to be sad, but it also really needed to happen. We haven't been very long-term goal-oriented for a long time, and I definitely think right now at this age we should be. Not in a desperate way, but my brain is like, *This is a path that will lead to something.*"

Before they knew Nick was losing his job, he and Muriel

booked a trip to Sicily, Italy. That's where Nick's family is from, but he hasn't been back in fifteen years, and Muriel's never been. They thought about going last year, but "we were dragging our feet," Nick says. "It was like, *We can't afford it. We can't justify it.*"

After they booked a commercial this year, they had some extra money. It could have gone to their credit card bill, but Muriel said, "Let's be irresponsible with it. Let's go to Italy."

They got into a film festival there to help justify the trip, then Nick's mom sent them $1,000. "Just do it," she said. "I know you're torn."

"It felt so generous," Nick says.

For the first time in his life, his parents have money to send him. His dad kept doing better and better as a director of business development in the waste-management industry, and the last ten years of his career had been particularly lucrative.

His parents didn't pay for his college or support him as an adult, but "now they're rich," Nick says.

When they get back from the trip, he won't have a job, but his dad told him, "Look, I know you want to get out of restaurants. If you need help with rent, if you need five thousand dollars, I'll send you five thousand dollars."

"We haven't taken it yet," Nick says. "I don't know if we will. It's a weird position to be in. It's all love, and he wants to be there for us. But I wasn't comfortable with it and neither was he."

He and Muriel talked about it for a while and decided that they would keep his dad's offer as an option. If they come back from Sicily, and he doesn't have an assistant job, he won't have to scramble for another restaurant job. "The idea is before we do anything drastic, I'm going to be a rich kid for a minute and take money from my dad," Nick says. "It was a weird thirty-five-year-old thing to go through, having that be offered. It was weird for him too."

For some thirtysomethings, getting financial assistance from your parents is common, a fact I think is widely known but hard to be open about, sort of like how no one talks about how they sometimes pee in the shower, even though that happens too.

"It's very difficult to admit help," says Chuck Collins, a scion of the Oscar Mayer food corporation and the author of *Born on Third Base: A One Percenter Makes the Case for Tackling Inequality, Bringing Wealth Home, and Committing to the Common Good.* "There's a fair amount of shame and a fair amount of incentive to omit those facts from your biography. Among close friends who are sharing an intimate conversation about their economic situations, people will acknowledge it, but we're all supposed to be self-made individual actors here."

Overall, one estimate predicts that boomers will ultimately pass along $30 trillion to their millennial children, whether that's by giving them money each month, a one-time gift, or providing them with free services they would have to otherwise pay for, like childcare. According to a 2018 report by Country Financial, a financial services firm in Bloomington, Illinois, more than half

(53 percent) of Americans ages twenty-one to thirty-seven have received some sort of financial assistance from a parent, guardian, or family member since turning twenty-one. This includes money for cell phone bills (41 percent), rent (40 percent), groceries and gas (32 percent), or health insurance (32 percent).

"The one thing to realize is there are all these not-very-big intergenerational transmissions of help," Collins says. "They don't have to be a trust fund. It could be, 'We bought a new car, you take the old car, and we'll pay your insurance for a year.' If we literally did the accounting maybe it would not add even up to $10,000. But even $4,000 or $5,000 of light subsidies can be a hedge against adversity. You don't want to overstate that this is a rich-kid phenomena. There are parents that have a lot more resources than they know what to do with. What better to do with it than to help your kids?"

Not everyone has this kind of privilege. Recipients of these kinds of gifts are most likely to be white and college educated, with well-paying jobs and some savings. In other words, they're more likely to already have financial advantages over other young adults.

"This generation is incredibly diverse," says Reid Cramer, the author of *The Emerging Millennial Wealth Gap* and fellow at the New America think tank, who focuses on the economic challenges facing young adults. "That's what's different from previous generations, but that's also what's leading to rising inequality. You'll have higher concentrations of people of color, and their wealth trajectory has been much lower than their white counterparts."

One of the major ways of building wealth is through homeownership, but many thirtysomethings can't save for a down payment on their own—debt is rising, wages are stagnant, and employment isn't secure. A recent economic analysis concluded, "For Americans under the age of 40, the 21st century has resembled one long recession." (And this study was done before the COVID-19 pandemic.)

Consequently, we have less overall wealth. This is a trend across all races and ethnicities, but white millennials have more wealth and own homes in greater percentages than Black and Hispanic households.

"There's a huge gap there," Cramer says.

The most recent wealth data from the Federal Reserve, in 2016, shows that the average wealth holdings of the typical Black millennial are approximately $5,700, compared to $26,100 for white millennials, while the typical Hispanic millennial had a net worth of $14,690.

I would not own a home in New York if my parents hadn't given me most of the money for the down payment on the one-bedroom apartment I bought in my midthirties. I was so proud the day I got the keys. It felt like an important accomplishment, having 650 square feet of space that was all mine. That night, I sat on the hardwood floor in my new apartment and drank sparkling wine from the bottle. But even as I celebrated what the apartment signified—I had my own space—I never wanted to hide that I had it because of my parents' gift.

Hannah Seligson wrote in the *New York Times* that there is a danger in not acknowledging this transfer of wealth: "It creates a distorted idea of what it takes to attain success and what financial milestones are actually achievable if you are starting from zero or less."

If someone knew I had this apartment, but didn't know that I didn't buy it all by myself, they might wonder what they were doing wrong. Why couldn't they save enough for their own down payment? Were they not working as hard as me?

No, the difference is: I got financial help from my parents, and not just with the apartment. They also paid for most of my college education and for a credit card that I used until I was in my early thirties. I want to demystify that what I have is what I earned—that always seems to be the default position in our society. If you're doing well, you deserve it. If you're struggling, something's wrong with you. I didn't do any more right or wrong than any other person. I had help.

"It would be so liberating for the culture for people to tell true stories about how they've made it or how they're surviving or not surviving," Collins says. "If we were more honest, maybe we could come together and find a collective solution, instead of these individual solutions. There's systemic things happening in the economy. These are not individual failings. But this is America. We blame ourselves."

———

In Sicily, the film festival Nick and Muriel got into was on a tiny, volcanic-rock island an hour boat ride from the main island.

Usually at festivals Muriel dutifully goes to all the panels, but at this one, "it was basically dudes from Palermo talking about *A Clockwork Orange*," she says. "We're on vacation. I'm not going to listen to these guys talk about movies for three hours." Instead, every day, they went snorkeling and, every night, they went to the open-air discotheques and danced under the stars and, occasionally, meteor showers. After the festival, they traveled to Casalvecchio Siculo, where Nick's family is from, which is on the top of a mountain and wasn't even marked on their map. It was so far removed from any reality Muriel knew. They climbed to a crumbling cemetery and around ancient, abandoned buildings. They dodged ash falling from the sky due to a fire at the cemetery. When they got locked out of their Airbnb, seemingly all of the villagers, led by Nick's distant cousin, came to help get them back in. "It was the most magical run-and-gun place," Muriel says.

Going back to Los Angeles was hard. Nick learned he could get unemployment, so he's doing that while he's interviewing for jobs at studios and production companies, but both of them are reevaluating their life in LA, trying to figure out if they're still happy making sacrifices to keep pursuing careers in comedy. "It was a reality check to be like, *If you're thirty-six, how much longer do I want to live where I don't get to feel the way I felt when I was in Sicily?*" Muriel says. "Some people have real downtime and build families and have vacation and all that stuff that we don't. It was always like, *Oh, I don't care about that.* But is what I felt in Sicily what that feels like? Do you feel free and light?"

Nick went on an interview for an assistant job at a production company he was really excited about—it's responsible for one of his favorite shows. The producer told him specifically that he was looking for people who wanted to move up; one of his directors started as an assistant.

"I was, like, salivating," he says. He treats interviews the same way he does his stand-up; he tries to be genuine and vulnerable, and make a connection with his audience. When the producer asked, "Where do you see yourself in five years?" Nick answered, "Well, to be honest, that's really in flux for me right now."

Nick thought the interview was a success and that the producer appreciated his honesty.

As he waits to hear back about the job, he's been doing more stand-up, going four to five times a week, often during the day to open mics that start at 11:00 a.m. "You're just doing jokes for other comedians, which is both really helpful and a fate worse than death for sure," Nick says. "Part of it is, *Well, what am I doing?* Stand-up for me just feels like instant gratification. My joke book is this secret I have in my pocket. At any time, I can come up with material I care about. It's not a safety net in an income way, but it feels good to do it."

He's working on making his routine more conversational, about what he's going through in the moment, while also landing his planned jokes. One of his bits is about being jealous of his friends who are surpassing him in their careers, "just classic bitter shit," he says.

The joke starts: *Okay, people say there's no seasons in LA. I grew up in Seattle, and I get it.*

Nick continues: *But there are seasons. It's still hot, but the leaves are changing and two more of my friends I started comedy with just got nominated for Emmys and three more got hired at* SNL.

Then, the punchline: *You remember that guy who got hired there then immediately got fired for that racist Asian joke? My first thought was, Please God, let that have been one of my friends.*

"Stand-up feels good when I'm being truthful," Nick says, "so just the act of being truthful in that stuff is usually helpful, generically speaking. It's knowing that negative things have the power to be positive because you can turn them into a joke. I don't know that I'm like the type of person who exorcises his demons onstage. I don't know if I really relate to that, but I definitely feel more alive and powerful over negative things."

———

Nick's unemployment runs out soon. He knows that after that his dad would give him rent money, but he doesn't want to take it, both because he and his dad are uncomfortable with the arrangement and because his dad assumed it would take him only a month to find the kind of assistant position he was after. "He was like, *Just do it for a month until you get a job you like,* which is a beautiful gift, but I kind of knew it then and I absolutely know it now, to get a job I like in this industry is going to take more time," Nick says. "Floating me for a month, as generous as that is, is not going to do it."

Nick's parents used to be artists too, when they lived in New

York City. His dad was a jazz musician, and his mom was an actor. They could survive on this work alone. His dad got paid $50 for one gig, which was enough for the rent on their squalid apartment. Then when they turned thirty, Nick was born and they moved to Seattle, where his dad went to work in an office, and his mom took care of Nick. Eventually, they bought a house and had two more kids.

Now, his dad watches what Nick is doing and is wistful for his days as a jazz musician. He tells Nick all the time, "You're living the dream." From his point of view, Nick and Muriel don't have anything to worry about: They make stuff they like. They hang out with their friends. They don't have kids. "But what they don't see is that we can't use our health insurance because it's so expensive," Nick says. "Apartments are no longer cheap. It's not easy to do this anymore. That quality of life has diminished so much."

Nick tries to tell his dad that this isn't their dream. "We're not satisfied with our careers and our standing and capabilities, and we want to keep striving," he says.

His dad dismisses this, "Nah, you're living the dream."

Nick never heard back from the interview that he thought went well, even after he sent a few follow-up emails. "I couldn't get a response out of them," he says. Since then he's been applying for five to ten jobs a week, but hasn't gotten any other interviews and feels like he's getting kicked around a little bit. With Muriel, he's trying to figure out what to do next. Maybe he should stop looking for assistant jobs? Maybe he should go back to working at a restaurant? Maybe he should go all out auditioning for commercials? Maybe he and Muriel should write another web series? How can they go after the careers they want without wrecking the life they have? "It's like gambling," he says. "If you win, the payday is great. But you're gambling with your literal life. This is my time on earth, and this is my life."

––––––––––

It's December and solidly winter in Grand Rapids. Adam has to contend with the snow and sickness that's everywhere. He and the rest of his family have colds, but "I think my body knows it can't get too sick," he says. "I have to keep the household running. I can't stay in bed all day."

Each weekday morning, he gets the girls dressed and makes his oldest daughter lunch. Then they all get in the car to take his oldest daughter to kindergarten. Lately, she hasn't wanted him to leave her there. "It doesn't surprise me," he says. "She's always been a sensitive kid. It just means that I have to deal with my crying child clinging to my legs as I walk out the door."

The rest of the day is spent back at the house with his youngest daughter: watching the cartoon show *Adventure Time*, chewing only the top crusts off her peanut butter sandwiches, doling out oatmeal cookies, and helping her find her teddy bear, Sugar Bear, whenever he goes missing. She's strong-willed, and the two of them often annoy each other. "There's nowhere else for that will to go except to crash up against me," he says. "But all of that stuff feels normal. It's the snow I have to wade through on a daily basis."

He compares his role in his household to being at the front of the line in *Final Fantasy*, a role-playing video game where each player in a monster-fighting group takes turns absorbing the damage from the monsters so the rest of the players can "cast spells or attack or whatever," he says. In this case the monster is domestic life, and he's always the one at the front, taking the blows from tantrums, messes, and never-ending cooking and cleaning, so "that gives my wife the time and space to gather gold," he says. "In a certain sense it's unequal, in that I do more of the home-life duties than my wife, but that's how we've agreed to run our home and live our lives."

Absorbing the damage has been wearing on him recently though, making him grumpier than usual, possibly because he turns thirty-seven in a few weeks, and the birthday puts him officially in his late thirties. "That feels very close to forty," he says, "and forty feels like a significant milestone in terms of development. It's a very clear timeline that you can mark things you have done and haven't done. I always thought that by devoting myself to being a stay-at-home dad and a writer, my life would look less conventional than if I was working an office job and that wouldn't bother me. I would be following this life and not having a lot to show for it. But I still feel very accountable to those standards of conventionality. I'm not as special as I thought I was." When he goes to his wife's annual family reunion in July, it bothers him that he has less to talk about than the other men there.

He submitted the novel he'd been trying to find an agent for to a contest at a literary magazine, hopefully to get some attention for it, but it didn't win. The defeat seemed like the final sign he should stop trying to get the book published. "Trying to get writing placed is a discouraging process, and I worry that I'm not very good at it," he says. "I feel very distant from the whole process. I thought that the book had more commercial appeal, all of which is to say, going back to what I said about feeling distant, when I try to figure out what constitutes commercial appeal, I have no idea what people want."

He's starting a new book, but beginning the project now has him reckoning with a timeline he never anticipated when he dreamed of being a writer as a kid: if he does become a published author, he will most likely be over forty when he does. "That's just not how I imagined myself," he says. "I'll never be a young debut writer, which is a weird thought. It was a youthful dream. I thought it would happen within the realm of my youth, and now I wonder if it was one of those dreams I should have left behind in childhood or adolescence."

As the year comes to an end, Adam is still mentally adjusting his imagined career trajectory, but he also got a small relief: his oldest daughter has returned to being calm when he drops her off at kindergarten. "I knew she was going to get back to that," he says. "It just took a while." Sometimes she wants him to walk her to the classroom, other times she wants to be left at the curb, but no matter what, they always say goodbye the same way: with a high five, a fist bump, and a hug and kiss. Then they repeat the whole sequence.

His parents and in-laws came to visit too, to see his daughters in their school holiday pageant, and it went well. At dinner one night, while the whole family was in the dining room, they complimented him on the improvements he's made to the house, like putting in a new kitchen floor. Adam still noticed the house was kind of messy and that they had yet to unpack a few boxes from the move, but "it was a nice moment," he says. "It was this moment of feeling like our parents thought we were doing a good job at life in general. We have a house. My wife has a decent job, and I can take care of the kids. I worry a lot about, *I haven't done these things* or *There's stuff I still need to do*, but I have done some things right. It was a nice feeling to have, that sense of we're doing all right. So many moments lately have felt fraught or anxious. Those are emotions I find easy to access, but that sense of contentment or pride or satisfaction, I don't feel that very often."

———

On Adam's birthday at the end of January, his wife took care of their daughters for the afternoon so he could go see a movie by himself. He watched *Monrovia, Indiana*, a documentary about life in the small town. "It was fun to pay attention to something that closely for that long," he says, unlike on normal afternoons when his youngest daughter requests something from him every five minutes, usually a snack.

For most of his thirties, he's been a stay-at-home dad, but he hasn't thought of being a father as a huge part of his identity. "It's mostly the way I relate to my kids and my wife," he says. "It's this internal domestic thing." But the other day he was talking to another parent about setting up a playdate for their daughters and realized that as he gets older and his kids get older, "the dadness part of myself gets extended further into the world beyond my home."

He started another novel, writing he knows is important to do for himself, no matter if it never has another audience. "If my brain isn't occupied with a big project, I start spinning my wheels and dwelling on thoughts that make me anxious and nervous," he says. "It's not good for me to have that much mentally empty room."

To that end, he also started a weekly email newsletter, called *Very Distant Lands*, where he writes about fatherhood and pop culture.

In the second one he wrote about *Breaking Bad*, a drama about Walter White, a teacher and father who turns into a meth dealer. Adam describes a scene where White shows his newborn baby the stacks of cash he has hidden in the garage. "I did this for you," he tells the baby.

Once, Adam thought he'd accomplish the same thing with his novels that White has with meth: making extra money for his family. But he hasn't been able to do that so far. And, he wrote in the newsletter, maybe that's okay:

I still think my kids have gained something from seeing me scribbling in my legal pads. Someone once told me that children seeing their parents devote themselves to an art is valuable, demonstrating the patience and attention that humans are capable of when they pursue something they love.

He's been thinking about next year when both of his daughters will be in school and he'll have the house to himself for long stretches, "which seems crazy to me," he says. Then he might get a part-time job, possibly at a grocery store where a friend works, while still working on his novel at night. It would get him out of the house and help him contribute financially. Plus, unlike with writing, it would give him immediate gratification. He'd show up, do his work, and leave.

Then, one night when both kids were in bed, his wife asked if they could talk. Without any preamble, she said, "I've been thinking we should try for another baby. What do you think?"

Adam had been thinking about this himself but hadn't said anything. Bringing it up with his wife felt like jinxing the comfortable, relatively anchored life they had going. "But as soon as she said it, it was like, *Yes, I'm ready*," he says. "I was ready right then and there." It would mean he wouldn't be getting a part-time job, since he'd be busy taking care of the new baby, but "I was willing, happy even, to do that," he says. "I'm ready to go back to those sleepless nights and those early two years of craziness."

Having three kids seemed perfect to him, and the timing felt right. His days would be laid out with his wife at work, his two daughters at school, and him at home with the new baby. This was a good plan.

It *was* a good plan, but when they were ready to start trying for another baby, the college his wife works for announced that not as many students had enrolled as it expected, and it was going to have to get rid of some positions, possibly hers. The cuts wouldn't be announced until May, which was four months away.

"We don't know one way or another," Adam says. "The job that we moved up here for and bought a house for may fall through."

They put their plan to try for a third baby on hold. They're not sure what kind of insurance, if any, they'll have in a few months. His wife and her coworkers now work with their belongings packed in boxes at their desks so they can leave without too much of a scene if they are asked to. Just as Adam was starting to feel some kind of settled in his life, it might all be upended.

"We thought we finally caught a break," he says. "Maybe it's possible things will stay stable, and we will continue on the path we thought we were on, but it's possible we won't. It's a reminder that things are never going to be that stable."

CHAPTER FIVE

Having a Child

---

*A lot of people tell me that life just sorts itself
and I need to stop trying to plan.*

—ABIGAIL

Muriel has a friend who is a year older than she is, single, and would like to have kids someday. She went to the doctor to talk about her fertility, and the doctor told her the best thing for her to do would be to freeze her eggs soon. "We were both kind of shocked," Muriel says. "We're the same age. I assumed I've got a few more years of fertility, and to see that your eggs are just aging."

Muriel hasn't decided if she wants kids or not, ambivalence that makes her feel guilty. Her mom was twenty-four when she had Muriel. "I'm twelve years older than that, and I still don't know," Muriel says. Her mom, who's a painter, had three more kids after Muriel too. "My mom loves having babies," Muriel says.

She always gave birth at home, and her midwife took pictures. Over the years, the slides of the births got mixed in with the pictures of Muriel's mom's paintings, "so you're flipping through the art and then all of sudden there's like a picture of me crowning," Muriel says. "It's so horrific."

She has friends who are sure they want kids, others who are positive they don't, but she never talks to anyone who is uncertain, like her. The lack of discussion about this makes her paranoid about not having an answer. "It feels like an issue or a problem, like I'm being bad," she says. "It's like, *Are you a child? You don't know whether you want to have kids? How do you not know at this age?*"

Because she feels so guilty about her uncertainty, she leans toward it meaning she shouldn't have kids. If she doesn't know by now if she wants them, she doesn't deserve them and wouldn't be a good mom anyway.

She and Nick keep talking about it.

"I don't know what I want," Muriel tells him. "What do you want? Do you want to do this?"

Nick says, "Yeah, let's have a baby."

"But it doesn't feel intentionally enthusiastic," Muriel says. "It's wishy-washy."

Nick suggested she stop taking birth control on her thirty-sixth birthday, which is in a week. She countered that they start trying in another year, when they'd be thirty-seven and thirty-eight, but she knows that she's just pushing it back because she's not sure what she wants. "We're not really planning it," she says. "If we're not enthusiastic and on board, we're not changing our lives to accommodate a kid. I'm pretty intentional when I want to make something happen. Right now, I'm more about, *I like my apartment. I'm not going to move to Burbank.*"

Nick is more definite about wanting kids someday but feels like he hasn't accomplished enough to be a happy parent yet. It's not that he hasn't made enough money. He'd be fine raising a child in their one-bedroom apartment with their one car, "everything normal except we'd be even broker because of our kid," he says. But what he doesn't want to do is raise a child while his career still feels unformed. Sometimes, though, he wishes he and Muriel had just had kids when they were twenty. "They'd be teenagers now," he says. "When I think about having children, my age doesn't feel arbitrary. I feel like a human being whose body is dealing with this thing called time."

———

In 2019, the birth rate in the United States fell for a fifth straight year and reached the lowest it's been in thirty-five years, according to a government report done by the Centers for Disease Control and Prevention. This means that close to six million babies who would have existed if the birth rates had stayed flat aren't being born.

The trend is surprising demographers, who assumed that these births were simply postponed because of the Great Recession of 2008. After the economy recovered, the birth rates would increase again, as they did during the baby boom that happened after the Great Depression in the twenties and thirties. The young adults who'd been stalled in starting their careers and marrying would start to have children.

"Every year, I expect the fertility rates to go up, and every year they go down," says Kenneth M. Johnson, a demographer at the University of New Hampshire. "I'm beginning to wonder if a significant number of these births won't occur. Maybe they're not delayed at all."

Demographers say that the stay-at-home orders during the coronavirus pandemic won't cause the birth rate to jump either, even though couples are stuck inside together. The idea of baby booms happening after disasters like blizzards or blackouts is a myth, and the pandemic is more likely to delay or discourage people from having children. "I really don't think they're saying, 'Oh, let's have a baby in the midst of the greatest epidemic that the country has faced in one hundred years,'" Johnson says.

Adam's wife didn't lose her job and, during the coronavirus pandemic, found herself a more vital part of the university she works at since it's her responsibility to convey information to the public about how the school is addressing the virus. "In a weird sense, she has the most job security she's ever had," Adam says.

But with his wife working more hours, now from their bedroom, and Adam taking care of the kids in the rest of the house, they're stressed, seeing less of each other than before, and not in an emotional state where they can fathom having another kid.

"We're tired," Adam says. "My wife is working really hard, with a lot more than usual to do, and I try to keep the kids occupied. Although meltdowns are infrequent, both children and adults, it's just, a lot. When people talk to me about a baby boom happening because of the pandemic, it's like, *Are you fucking kidding me?*"

———

Abigail, who's thirty-four and lives in Nashville, first asked her gynecologist about freezing her eggs eight years ago, when she was twenty-six. "I grew up thinking that I would have a family someday," she says. "I was fully expecting to have a husband and a few kids." So when she was single and childless at twenty-six, she inquired about freezing her eggs. Her doctor laughed and told her to wait. "You don't need to worry about that until you're thirty-four," he said.

Abigail thought, *Thank goodness I won't be in this position at thirty-four.* By then, she'd be well on her way to the husband-and-children future she envisioned.

But in her thirties so far, she's had a couple of relationships that lasted a few months but "nothing super significant or of note," she says.

Her career has advanced more quickly than any relationship; she's now a national account manager for Coca-Cola, overseeing how the products are displayed in Dollar General chain stores. "I focused on that," she says, "but I don't want to say that's why I'm not married. I think people hear what I do and see the companies I've worked for, and they assume that I'm some ball-busting career woman and that's what I want. In reality, I would be just as satisfied having less in that life and having more on the personal front."

As she's gotten older, though, dating has felt more fraught, as if she can't spend a couple of months hanging out with a guy if she isn't sure he's the person she's going to have a family with. "Everyone tells you your clock is ticking," she says. "It didn't seem like I could have fun anymore. I had to be on mission, but I couldn't walk into a date and say, 'Hey, are you marriage material or not?'"

So, as soon as she turned thirty-four—the age that had been planted in her head for the past eight years—she went back to the doctor, ready to freeze her eggs.

That way she could keep dating without trying to figure out if the dude in front of her would be a good dad while they were having their first glass of wine together.

It would also give her some space to sit with a new idea: Lately she'd been thinking she might want to have a child *before* meeting her spouse.

While she was looking into freezing her eggs, she also considered doing an insemination with donor sperm, but in the end, "I wasn't ready to commit to that," she says. "There have been times when I have thought, *I really want to be a mom more than a wife*, but I'm not sure that's something I always feel. It's a lot of work, and having someone to share that would make it better and, even more than that, it would be nice having someone to share in special moments."

Abigail was raised in Nashville and speaks with a Southern accent. Her family still lives there, and she has lots of friends in town, but she didn't know anyone who'd frozen their eggs. "It's part of being in the South," Abigail says. "People don't talk about this stuff ever." She told some friends she was doing it. They were supportive, but couldn't relate. "Ninety-eight percent of my friends are married with kids, or have kids and are divorced," she says.

Recently, she went to a party where she didn't know many people, and everyone kept asking her if her kids went to school with the host's kids. She kept having to repeat that she didn't have kids. "It's not a big deal, but it is just something that I'm surrounded by," she says. "I'm in that world."

Abigail assumed she could go through the egg-freezing process all by herself just fine, like she did with everything else in her life. "I think part of it was like, *Why wouldn't I?*" she says. "I go to all my doctor's appointments by myself."

She's disciplined and likes to be in control. She goes to 6:00 a.m. cardio-and-weights workout class four days a week (and goes to bed at 9:30 p.m. so she's not tired for class). On the weekend, she goes to the same class, but at 9:00 a.m. "I'm not a complete masochist," she says.

When she went for her first appointment at the fertility clinic, she was more nervous than she thought she would be. "You spend so much time worrying about getting pregnant accidentally," she says, "and then you're walking into an office where they could tell you you're not fertile."

She was relieved when the blood tests and ultrasound showed she should have plenty of eggs to freeze. Insurance would cover some of the cost of the procedure, but she would still be paying about $5,500. Right after Christmas, she would start the hormone shots to stimulate her ovaries (the goal is for the ovaries to develop multiple eggs in a month, instead of a single one like usual).

She'd be on a break from work and didn't think what she was about to go through would be that big of a deal. "The Real Housewives, who I assume are complete morons, do it," she says.

Her first clue that egg freezing was going to be more complicated than she thought, both logistically and emotionally, came during the introductory class, where she learned how to give herself the shots. "Because my situation was different than most, and I wasn't like a-couple-going-through-it-together type thing, I just went to a one-on-one session, where they taught me how to do the injections," she says. "And I realized, *Oh, this is twenty-three injections. The Real Housewives give themselves twenty-three injections just like I'm about to.*"

———

For a long time, I wasn't sure if I wanted a child, and I wasn't in a rush to figure it out. I *thought* a lot about the decision, but in an abstract way. In my midthirties, I started to do calculations with my age and how long I could possibly wait to try to get pregnant. They went like, *If I got pregnant in a year I'd be thirty-eight when the baby was born,* or *If I got pregnant in two years, I'd be thirty-nine.* I read lots of articles about women's fertility decreasing after thirty-five, but they didn't worry me much. I read an equal number of stories that said those statistics were overly scary and I knew plenty of women who'd had kids after thirty-five.

As I got closer to forty, I started to get nervous. The articles that said my fertility would plummet after forty stressed me out.

I tried to tell myself that every woman was different, that I might not even have been able to get pregnant in my twenties, and that there were other ways to have kids. But I also finally wanted to do something about trying to get pregnant besides just talking about it and running endless numbers in my head.

In the scope of what I could do with my life, whether to have a child is the decision I struggled with the most. I saw it as the only one I couldn't take back. What I did for work, who I dated, where I lived, even who I married, all of that could be undone if it turned out I'd made the wrong choice. But a child would always be mine. How could I know for sure that I wanted to raise someone?

As I got older and closer to an age when I assumed I'd no longer be able to be pregnant, I accepted that I couldn't know for sure, and even though I had some fear and uncertainty about having a child, I wanted to do it anyway. I didn't want to do it because I was supposed to, or because it would help make me an adult, but because it was an experience I wanted to have. I wanted to do this with my life.

I'd always told myself that I'd be comfortable being a single parent. I took care of my life myself. I should be able to do this on my own too. But after my failed proposal, when I was single and actually considering solo parenting, I knew—after a stretch of sleepless nights—that I didn't want to. I wanted to have a child with a partner.

I made an appointment for a consultation at an egg-freezing clinic. I'd spent so much of my life telling myself that I didn't know if I could get pregnant, which is true no matter how many initial tests doctors run on your fertility, but I'd also been avoiding exactly what I was doing: taking steps to make the idea of getting pregnant more actual. The more unformed I kept this goal, the easier it was to keep having kids as a potential that might happen someday, but not yet.

In the doctor's office, I had my blood drawn and saw what my ovaries looked like, which was truly shocking to me—all this time what was happening in my uterus seemed like such a mystery. I had been avoiding finding out what was going on in my own body and figuring out how to get pregnant for real. Now, in both my body and brain, I was moving toward trying to have a child.

I was a good candidate for freezing my eggs and made an appointment to start the process. But the more I thought about it, the less I wanted to wait. I didn't want to freeze my eggs, start dating, and hope to find someone I wanted to have a child with so I could use them.

I already knew who I wanted to have a child with. I hadn't stopped thinking about my ex-boyfriend. I felt the same way I did the night I'd proposed—and that night, we'd talked a lot about having children. He wanted to have children soon, too.

We'd kept in touch, through texts and emails, and I knew that his life had changed since I'd proposed. He was single and had been laid off from his job. I also knew he didn't like the city he was living in and was looking all over the country for a new job.

I thought he might want to come to New York. Maybe now he'd be more open to getting back together, to living with me, but

I didn't want him to if he wasn't interested in also trying to have a child.

I decided to call him to tell him I was planning to freeze my eggs. I hoped he'd tell me not to.

———

For about two weeks, Abigail gave herself a few shots in the stomach every night, and most mornings, went to the fertility clinic so her doctor could monitor how her body was responding to the drugs via blood tests and ultrasounds. The hormones made her feel lethargic and bloated. She also wasn't allowed to exercise or drink alcohol. "It was around New Year's, so socially it was like, *Wait a second*," she says.

Her friends who knew what she was doing asked questions out of curiosity, but Abigail didn't have anyone who could empathize with the emotional side of the process, and during her mornings at the fertility clinic all she saw were couples, which made her feel even more isolated. "In my mind at the time, they were all perfect couples and the most supportive individuals," she says. "I'm sure the grass isn't always greener, but when you're sitting there alone for your sixth transvaginal ultrasound in nine days, you're like, *It must be nice to have a little support system there.*"

She regretted not asking any of her friends to come with her to the appointments—she knew they would have been there for her. She told her parents and two brothers she was freezing her eggs, in part because they would be coming over to her house during the holidays and see that she had dozens of needles around. "It looked like a freaking nursing home," she says. But she also wanted to tell them as a warning: this was the first step in possibly having a child on her own.

She wanted them to be supportive, even though she and her family are Catholic, and the Church would want her to be married before having a child.

Abigail assumed her mom would be understanding, and she has been, even if she's also suggested that instead of Abigail freezing her eggs and using a sperm donor, she could just try to get pregnant from a one-night stand. She was more worried about what her dad would say, but he offered to do anything for her, whether she decided to have a baby on her own or wait.

The day before the procedure where her eggs would be taken out, Abigail's hormone levels dropped, which isn't supposed to happen. They're supposed to stabilize or keep going up. She worried the procedure wouldn't work and, that night, slept badly. She thought, *I must have made a mistake*, and *I've spent all this money for naught. I'm going to go in there and they won't be able to do anything and I'll have to start over.* She didn't know when she'd be able to go through this again. She'd arranged everything around the holidays so her daily doctor's appointments and the fact that she was feeling blah wouldn't be so obvious at work.

In the morning, her mom picked her up to take her to the doctor. Abigail was testy with her on the drive. But when they got there, the nurses helped her feel calmer, as did the doctor, who told her there was nothing they could do at this point. He would just do the procedure and see what happened. "Ordinarily that probably would have ticked me off, but on that morning it was exactly what I needed to hear," Abigail says.

In the end, everything went fine, and Abigail had thirty-six eggs to freeze. "Maybe I'll never use them," she says. "Maybe I'll use them with a partner, and maybe I'll use them to have a child on my own. I'm open to all of that."

What she's not open to is not having a child, and her stockpile of eggs makes her feel more certain that she will be able to, in whatever way she chooses. "When I left the doctor's office on the day of the retrieval, I told my mother that I felt like the weight of the world had been lifted off my shoulders," she says.

———

According to the 2019 data, the biggest decreases in the birth rates are for women in their teens and early twenties. Women in their early thirties now have more babies than women in their early twenties, and women in their late thirties and early forties were the only age groups whose birth rates increased.

Women aren't saying that they want to have fewer children, at least in surveys. "They mostly say they want to have two," Johnson says. "Their expectations appear to be the same as always. There's been no dramatic drop-off in what women say they want to have."

But there is no doubt that fewer babies are being born, and most likely, the decline reflects the social changes in America, including women staying single longer and prioritizing their careers, as well as their personal and economic independence, over having children. America's drop in birth rate mirrors the fertility patterns in Europe, Japan, and Korea, where the economic strength of the countries means fewer deaths in childhood, greater access to contraception, and women who have more education and work outside the home.

In the United States, heterosexual married couples tend to have similar educational and career backgrounds and, consequently, earn about the same amount of money, although husbands still make slightly more. But, on average, women's incomes drop substantially and immediately after the birth of the couple's first child.

A study done in November 2017 by the Census Bureau found that the wage difference between spouses doubles after they start having kids. This is entirely due to decreases in women's pay—after they become moms, the study found that women earn an average of $25,100 less than their husbands, and their incomes never fully recover. Men's wages, on the other hand, keep rising after they become fathers.

However, the study also found an exception to this trend: How old women are when they have their first child matters. If their first baby is born when they are between the ages of twenty-five and thirty-five—the prime career-building years—their pay never returns to where it was before they had a child, but if they give birth when they are younger than twenty-five or older than thirty-five, they eventually close the pay gap with their husbands.

"The issue, in general, comes down to time," Claire Cain

Miller wrote in the *New York Times* in an article about the study. "Children require a lot of it, especially in the years before they start school, and mothers spend disproportionately more time than fathers on childcare and related responsibilities. This seems to be particularly problematic for women building their careers, when they might have to work hardest and prove themselves most, and less so for women who have already established some seniority or who have not yet started careers."

In the 1970s, the country also saw birth rates drop. Women started to go to college in greater numbers, had access to reliable birth control, and began to talk openly about being in control of their own bodies. In a 1974 episode of the television program about the Bunker family, *All in the Family*, which reached forty million viewers, Gloria, the only child of Archie and Edith Bunker, argued, "Ma, I believe a woman is meant to be a person first and then maybe a mother. I don't need to give birth to a baby to make me feel useful!"

In 2019, Taylor Swift echoed Gloria in an interview with a German publication when she refused to answer a question about if she was thinking about having kids because of her impending thirtieth birthday. "I really do not think men are asked that question when they turn thirty," she said. "So I'm not going to answer that now."

"It's good that we're allowed to say, 'Hey, just so you know, we're more than incubators,'" she explained later to *People*. "You don't have to ask that of someone just because they're in their mid-20s and they're a female."

"To me, one of the fundamental decisions of women, and certainly men too, is the decision about having a child," Johnson says. "It's hard to think of anything more fundamental than that. It's one of the reasons why demographic indicators are so interesting to watch. If you want to see an indication that society has changed socially, watch the birth rates."

———

On the morning of Christmas Eve, Yasin's wife, Melanie, came out of the bathroom with a funny look on her face.

"What's wrong?" Yasin asked.

"Nothing," she said. "I'm fine."

She wanted to wait to tell him she was pregnant until New Year's Eve, the anniversary of when they met four years before. But, that afternoon, as she was driving their rental car to Connecticut, where they were going to spend the day with her family, she said, "I took a test this morning."

Immediately, Yasin started to cry, "and she hadn't even told me she was pregnant yet," he says. "I haven't ever been overcome with emotion like that, to have happy tears." He still doesn't feel ready to be a parent. He and his company have not had the financial success he's striving for. But like with all his decisions, Yasin presents himself outwardly as confident about what he's chosen, even if in his head he's unsure. Now that Melanie is pregnant, he's preparing to be a parent, despite it feeling hurried.

When he told his mom that Melanie was pregnant, she started

crying too—she had stopped asking when they were going to have kids. "I'm Turkish, so that's the way it is," he says. "At twenty-five, she had four kids, and I'm over here at thirty-one wondering what it's like to be a dad. I used to think, *I'm not ready yet, but I'll be ready at some point.* But the reality is we're living the reality right now."

Yasin becoming a dad might mean he has to stop heaping the majority of his money, hours, and energy on his start-up. But doing that might mean that he doesn't make it to where he wants to. What if this is as successful as he's going to be?

"The scariest day in my life will be the day I peaked," he says.

After quitting his banking job, he spent any money he had on his start-up. He didn't take a salary and tried to keep all his personal expenses low by sharing a one-bedroom apartment with a married couple and eating Pop-Tarts for breakfast and ramen for lunch. This mentality shifted a little after he got married. He's taken a small salary for the past two and a half years, and he and Melanie rent their own one-bedroom in Jersey City, New Jersey, but Melanie pays for the majority of their expenses so Yasin can take as little money as possible away from his business.

He spent the money he had saved for retirement on his company too. Right now his plan is to retire on what he sells this company for or, if he keeps running it, the money it makes him when it's actually making money. But he knows that, statistically, most companies fail in five years, "in which case I will be starting fresh as a thirtysomething-year-old with zero in retirement," he says, a predicament he is ignoring for now. "Future Yasin will handle that. Current-day me is not going to borrow tomorrow's problems."

Melanie was fine with how Yasin was allocating his money, "but now my choices will impact someone who had no say in what I decided," he says. "I know how much my parents sacrificed for me. When the kids are still young is when I need to be building a future for them and providing all of the things they want and need to achieve their full potential."

Despite this, he's not considering a drastic career change before the baby is born, like trying to return to a job that comes with more money and security—he still wants to achieve his dream of founding a successful business. Part of him knows it's not all up to him, and what happened to his dad hovers over him. As hard as he works, he can't guarantee that he can build the kind of company he wants, any more than his own father could. The business world is fickle, and there are some scenarios where you make it, others where you don't.

He's always had a voice in his head saying, *You're going to do something big.* "But whether it's my age, or the amount of stress, ups and downs, and pummeling I've received from the business world, I'm starting to question that voice," he says. "I wonder, *Is it going to happen?*"

———

I was nervous before I called my ex. I was about to ask him if he wanted to move to New York and try to have a child with me. It was a lot to bring up on a phone call with a guy who seemed more distant from me than ever before.

He was expecting me to call. I texted him a few days before to see when he'd be free. On a Sunday afternoon, we chatted a little about what we'd been up to since the last time we'd seen each other—the conversation was easier and flirtier than I expected. Then I forced myself to be direct. I still wanted to be with him, that hadn't changed, and I knew he was thinking about what he wanted, but I was also reckoning with wanting to have a child. I had an appointment to freeze my eggs, but I was hoping he might want to move to New York and do this with me instead. We talked for a long time. As we ended the call, he told me he needed to consider everything, but "it was really nice to hear your voice," he said. I thought there was a good chance he would say yes.

Shortly after this conversation, he did. He didn't move immediately. We saw each other twice before he brought all his stuff with him. When he arrived, it was with the understanding that we were going to make a home together and eventually try to have a child. We started by puzzling out how to be in the same place together, both in the physical space we were sharing and in what we wanted out of our lives. We'd been friends and dated on and off for a long time, but we'd never been so directly affected by each other. We had small differences, like me waking up immediately and him needing to snooze for what feels like four hundred times. And we had bigger ones, like me being optimistic and not wanting to worry about the future and him being more concerned with being practical and prepared for things that might go wrong. We talked a lot. We also fought. All of it moved us toward being able to align ourselves in the present.

I adore him. The other day, we were both coming home at the same time. I saw him on the street, and it made me full-body happy that he was there—and headed to the apartment we share. I hurried to catch up with him.

Whether I'm hanging out in the kitchen while he cooks, or we're roughhousing, which we've always done like children, or we're talking about something tough, our relationship feels like a partnership. It feels like we're connected and committed, in an authentic and secure way that I want to last forever.

I still want to marry him, but he thinks of marriage as more of a formality. This is one of the things we fought about. But he moved to the city I love because I asked him to, and, for now, our relationship feels right as it is.

A mutual friend once observed about us, "there's so much love there," which is true. Sometimes I'm giddy about him being here. It feels like magic that he is. But I also know it isn't. To come together, we had to take our relationship seriously. We had to grab each other's hands and agree to go the same way.

———

In about three months, Yasin will become a father. Before then, he's attempting to take advantage of not having a child to care for. "I don't want to see this period of my life, to look back on it, and say, *What did I do with this time?*" he says.

He and the brother he's closest to, who is three years younger than he is, planned a sixteen-day trip to Southeast Asia. They both love to travel but, in years, haven't spent much time together where it was just the two of them. His brother lives in Boston now, but even when he lived in New Jersey they saw each other irregularly. On the trip, they biked around Taipei; explored Bangkok, Phuket, and Kuala Lumpur; and hiked in Hong Kong, "the hardest hike of my life," Yasin says, "but I was like, 'I can't give up now. No one's gonna come get me.'"

Yasin's favorite night was near the end, in Kuala Lumpur. Malaysia is more than 60 percent Muslim, and he and his brother hadn't been in a majority Muslim country since they were kids visiting Turkey with their parents. That night they got back to their hotel around seven, after sightseeing all day.

Ramadan, the most sacred period of the year in the Muslim religion, was about to start. They'd be heading home for a month of fasting, prayer, and reflection, so they decided to listen to a lecture about Islam. "We wanted to reset the moral compass," Yasin says. "I use religion as a guide for how to be a good person, to be better than the day before, and to be a good member of the community."

He and Melanie are going to raise their baby, who they learned is a girl, and any other kids they have in the Muslim faith. "I want to give them enough examples of what a good Muslim is," he says. "They have plenty of examples of what bad Muslims are in the media. But you can't control someone else's religion. When they're out of the house, they can decide for themselves."

When he was little, his mom sent him and his three brothers to camp to learn about Islam and be around other people who were Muslim. "In the US that concept is foreign because it's not a

Muslim society," he says. "A lot of people don't get that until they get to college."

In Kuala Lumpur, he and his brother had intended to go back out for dinner, but after the lecture, they ended up sitting in bed talking: about life, their aspirations, and what their roles should be in the world. "We traveled halfway across the world, close to the equator, so we could have a conversation about love, morals, family, career, and death," he says.

While they talked, the curtains were open. They watched the sky get dark and the lights of the city come through the window. There were six tall skyscrapers in the background, lit in blues and purples. Eventually, they opened a box of desserts they'd gotten in Taipei and ate them, even though it was supposed to be a gift for their family back home. Around midnight, the pauses between their thoughts started to get longer, and they fell asleep, unsure who'd spoken last.

"The thing I remember most is the feeling of it," Yasin says. "It was cathartic."

His life doesn't look like how he imagined it would before he brought another person into the world. When he was a teenager thinking about who he'd be when he had his first child, he assumed he'd be "twenty-seven or twenty-eight," married, and already a millionaire. Whenever he and his wife weren't working, they would go to fancy cocktail parties and dinners, part of "a nerdy Ivy League–type scene, where we'd talk about the fourth dimension with physicists," he says. "My wife would be more impressive than I was, and I would be very impressive."

In reality, he's thirty-one, and he and Melanie just moved into a two-bedroom apartment, the first time he's lived in a place with two bedrooms in his adult life, "and I am expecting a kid while I work from home on a sports app," he says.

When he looks around their new apartment, he's bewildered by the baby books and stuffed animals that weren't there two months ago.

Still, no matter what he envisioned, he's not as intimidated by the next twenty-four months as he is by the next twenty-four years. "The start of the race seems manageable to me," he says. "There's a lot more gray in the next twenty-four years. I think about making sure I can be a good example and raising kids who feel that they are capable. I don't want to limit what they can do."

When he got home to Jersey City, Ramadan started. Usually during it, he gets up at 3:45 a.m. to make breakfast. He eats quickly, then goes back to sleep, but this year, he hasn't been able to fall back asleep. He was still jet-lagged from the trip, plus Melanie was on her last business trip before she gives birth, and "when she's not around, I don't sleep well," he says.

He's never thought of himself as someone who follows gender roles. He and Melanie split chores, she does the laundry and he does the dishes—he thinks of them as equal partners. But with the pregnancy, he feels like she's doing more, and "I feel guilty about that," he says. (Before he left on his trip, he did go to the grocery store to stock up on Melanie's favorite foods, then hid notes for her all over the house. "I thought about where she'd be so it wouldn't be just a rush of notes the day I left," he says. "I went to the third cereal box, not the one that's open now, so she'd get it toward the end of my trip.")

Melanie has researched baby gear and has preferences for a dresser, car seat, stroller, and crib, and "I'm like, 'We'll figure that out when the baby is closer to here,'" he says. "But it's physically affecting her. The time for her is right now."

The other day, she asked him to talk to her belly, to say something to the baby, but "it feels weird to me to do that," he said.

"It's so real to you," he told her, "and it's real to me, but not in the same sense."

———

A few weeks after freezing her eggs, Abigail went for her annual checkup with her gynecologist. They discussed if Abigail wanted to renew her birth-control prescription. She did, but temporarily.

"When I come back in a year, I might be ready to move forward with having a child," she said.

She surprised herself a little with this answer. She knew she was feeling that way, but she hadn't expected to say it aloud. Telling her gynecologist about her desire, and that she planned to act on it soon, moved it from inside her head to "out in the universe," she says. "Thinking something and saying something are two very different things."

Abigail's not totally sure that in a year she will be ready to try to have a child on her own, and she's open to not doing it if she meets someone she wants to co-parent with. Then she'd be comfortable waiting another couple of years to have a child because she has her eggs frozen. Still, she's making some preparations for having a child soon, and on her own, including moving to a bigger house. When she was thirty, she bought "my big-kid house," she says about her one-story blue bungalow with three columns, a wraparound porch, and a yard. She's crazy about it, but it's small, with no room for a nursery, so "I started to think I need to get my ducks in a row," she says. "The next chapter of my life is going to include a little person."

At the local bakery she goes to some mornings on her way home from the gym ("because that makes sense," she says), she told the owner she might be looking for a new home, and the owner recommended a Realtor. When Abigail met the Realtor, she asked him to show her homes only in the same area she currently lives in, because it's zoned for a very good elementary school.

"I felt like a lunatic," she says. "I was asking for a child that didn't exist and might not, but he said that he totally understood."

Within three weeks, Abigail was in the process of buying a four-bedroom house that's almost twice the size of the bungalow. She was planning to get a smaller house, "but you can't help what you fall for," she says. There is a room in the house that she thinks will be the nursery, but, for now, it will be a guest room. Filling it with baby furniture before she's sure about having a child on her own "would be putting the cart before the horse," she says.

Abigail also announced on her Facebook and Instagram accounts that she'd frozen her eggs. She posted a photo of herself in the hospital bed, thumbs up and smiling after she learned the procedure had been successful. "I have debated making this post for the last two weeks," she wrote in the caption. "On one hand it is deeply personal and on the other, I want to help people like me. So here I am oversharing on social media in hopes that someone feels a little bit less alone down the road."

She didn't know what kind of reaction she'd get—"I definitely held my breath and hit send," she says—but all the messages were positive. Friends congratulated her. Acquaintances told her they were considering freezing their eggs and asked questions. A former coworker wrote to say that she'd had a child on her own and invited Abigail to her house to meet her newborn daughter. They spent time catching up, but they also talked, in detail, about how the woman picked her donor sperm. "Seeing her at complete ease with her new life as a single mom was very reassuring for me," Abigail says. "It made it all seem feasible." She left the visit inspired.

Her former coworker also told her about a Facebook group for women who've had kids on their own. Abigail read the thread for hours. She was surprised, and comforted, to see many women in her area in the group. "I thought, I live in Nashville, Tennessee, and there was no one doing it, but that's not true," she says. The women were honest about how difficult it is to have a child alone and answered some questions Abigail had about sperm donors. They also brought up issues she hadn't thought of, such as, *How do you bring the baby home from the hospital?*

"Usually your partner would do it, but you don't have one to take you," Abigail says. "One woman was worried, *How am I going to drive home?*"

Abigail hasn't really been dating, partly because she prefers to stay home in the winter, what she calls her "hibernation mode." But freezing her eggs also made her feel empowered that "I don't need a man to do this," she says. "I do want a partner. I do want a husband, but I don't have to have that." The point of freezing her eggs was to give her more time before she tried to get pregnant, but "instead it made me excited about the next steps," she says. "I was talking with someone about this today, and they said, 'You have to roll with it.'"

As it got warmer out, she did say yes when a friend from her gym wanted to set her up on a blind date. The guy was nice, but Abigail didn't feel any great connection with him. They went out a few times after their first meeting, but he was finishing a master's degree, she was closing on her new house, and neither was that motivated to keep scheduling time to see each other. So they just stopped making plans, and Abigail has no regrets. "He won't go down as a missed opportunity," she says. "I'm not longing for anything."

She doesn't like dating, and loathes dating apps. Instead, she prefers to hang out at backyard barbecues or at the lake with her close friends, most of whom have kids. Often, in the evenings, she goes back to her old neighborhood to sit on her former neighbors' porch and eat Popsicles with their toddlers.

"I've had the conversation with everyone that I've got to be intentional about these things," she says. "I need to stop expecting the UPS man to be the man of my dreams. I don't have to go out to bars with my single friends. I have to get back on the apps, but I wish there was a better way."

She keeps imagining what her days would be like if she were raising a child alone, mentally noting what gyms have daycare facilities or where the playgrounds are in her new neighborhood. She also visualizes her life if she were married with a child. "It's the same sort of images, but you'd have two sets of hands to wrangle versus one," she says.

She continues to want to make a decision about trying to get pregnant on her own by the new year—a year from when she froze her eggs. "I don't want to say it's top of mind, but it's definitely top quadrant," she says.

Abigail loves to do research and will go deep digging up information on anything she's interested in. She spent hours looking into the process of choosing sperm and scanning the reviews of different clinics. She talked with her neighbors about preschools and ended up reading about "curriculums and school zones and crap that doesn't affect me," she says. She saved an article from British *Elle* called "Why I Became a Single Mum Using a Sperm Donor Aged 37."

But she's also unsure if she wants to stay at her job with Coca-Cola for much longer. Eleven years ago, in 2008, she wanted to become a real estate agent. She took a course to get her license and passed the test, but this was during the Great Recession and the nationwide collapse of the housing market, and "I wasn't brave enough to go into it at that point," she says. So, instead, she started working in the consumer-packaged goods industry.

Now she's thinking about taking the test again. Buying the new house reinvigorated her interest in real estate. Part of her thinks it would be foolish to leave her job. If she was going to be a single mom, she'd need her salary and benefits. But she's also increasingly aware she's not passionate about her career. She's done well at it because she wants to do well at everything she takes on, and she enjoys having enough money to make big purchases like her new house. But in the long term, does she really want to raise a child while doing work she doesn't care about? Would her discontent seep into her parenting?

Some of what's motivating her wanting to make a big change is that she's about to turn thirty-five. Her birthday is on August 20, but she celebrates the whole month, which she renames Abigust. "I want to be in a place where I'm happy and doing something that I feel like provides value," she says. "I'm not where I want to be at thirty-five. I'm where I want to be from the house I live in, from a stuff perspective, but stuff doesn't matter."

As she's been struggling with this, her former colleague who had a child on her own texted: "Are you pregnant yet?"

"Peer pressure has changed a lot," Abigail says. "It used to be, like, *Go out on a Tuesday.*"

———

At Yasin and Melanie's, the nursery is ready. There's a crib, a dresser, a changing station, a lamp, a rocking chair, and, in the corner, a desk for Yasin. The baby is due at the beginning of football season, which is his busiest time at work. He doesn't get an official paternity leave but is planning to work odd hours after the baby is born. He survived a yearslong run of getting very little rest while he was launching his business, so he thinks he can handle this period of sleep deprivation too, "but it's a different challenge," he says. "It's more of an emotional, *I want to be there for my baby.* I don't want to miss out on the few months of our baby being a baby."

He and Melanie took a class on what to expect during the birth, and Yasin was surprised to learn that he is supposed to snip the umbilical cord, which he doesn't want to do. "Apparently, it feels rubbery," he says. "I'm going to be weirded out when I feel how rubbery it is, and I realize there's no feeling there, but there's something about cutting something that was part of your wife's and child's bodies."

Four days before the baby's due date, Melanie and Yasin arrived at the hospital, around 8:00 p.m., pretty sure Melanie was in labor. "It's very confusing," Yasin says. "When she started having contractions, we'd be like, *Is this real labor?*" The baby girl they named Leyla arrived the next day, around 4:30 p.m., and had so much thick black hair that the doctor commented on it as she was delivering her. Yasin was observing everything, but, even as he was, he still felt like the baby wasn't real.

"The first minute or two the baby's an alien to you," he says. "You don't know who that person is. They don't look like a person. It's an anonymous face, like a clay model of what a baby should be."

The doctor asked him, "Are you ready to cut the cord?"

"Yes," Yasin said.

"Do you want a picture?" a nurse asked.

"Yes," Yasin said again.

The nurse kept standing there, amused, but Yasin wasn't sure why. He said he wanted a photo.

Finally the nurse said, "Well, get your phone, then."

He cut the cord in a single snip, which made him proud. "That doesn't always happen," he says. About ten minutes later, he held his daughter for the first time. According to Islam, when babies are born, you're supposed to recite the call to prayer to them, "so I did that in her ear," Yasin says.

Two days later, he texted me more about the birth:

"I'm tired and in love."

"She has so much hair."

"Here's a telling photo tho," he wrote.

In it, he was standing in the hospital room, holding his new baby with one hand while typing on his laptop with his other.

———

Abigail kept thinking about quitting her job at Coca-Cola to be a Realtor. She repeated the class to get her license and passed the test again, but spent a few weeks after she did unsure about making the career change, stuck weighing the same pros and cons she had eleven years ago. But in early August, "I flipped the switch that I was going to do it," she says. "It wasn't a shock that I *wanted* to do it"—her family and friends knew she'd been considering it—"but the fact that I actually did it, that was shocking."

She's prepared to go six months living on savings. The real estate firm she joined told her that, at minimum, she will have sixty to ninety days without any income, an amount of time she calls "insane." After that, it will probably take six more months to get regular sales. "It could be more," she says, "but I'm not working from that school of thought. I'm not allowing myself to go there."

She's excited about how her new job may shake up her life and take her out of the routine of early-morning workouts and early bedtimes she's been in. Part of being a Realtor is to be super social, always up for meeting potential clients by going out all the time and talking with strangers (instead of avoiding eye contact with them like Abigail had been doing).

"I was getting kind of complacent," she says. "I was going through the motions and wasn't stepping outside of my comfort zone and making any real effort. This will force me into other social settings and get me out of the house."

Her career change has pushed back her timeline for having a child on her own, but perhaps not by that long, maybe eight or nine months, "maybe just six months," Abigail says. "I thought I'd have it figured out by the beginning of the year, and I would have loved to have done that, but I don't feel like, with me being so unhappy at work, it would have been a good thing for me or for the baby."

When she told her grandma she was becoming a Realtor, the first thing her grandma asked was, "What does this mean about my great-grandbaby?"

"That breaks my heart a little bit," Abigail says, "because she's eighty-five. I'm her favorite grandchild. She doesn't care about the approach. She just wants it to happen."

Abigail does too. The other day she got a letter from the facility that's storing her eggs. It offered her a cheaper rate if she moved them from Nashville to somewhere in Nevada. She declined. "I want to keep them close," she says.

On her thirty-fifth birthday, she had a party at her new house, with tacos, burritos, and tequila, and was really happy the whole night. On past birthdays, she's thought about what she doesn't have, but this year she thought about what she does: eggs she knows are younger than she is, a house she's in love with, and a new career she's eager to get started in. "I feel really good about thirty-five," she says. "I have no idea why. I've kind of regressed in a big way, like, *Wait a second, you're going backwards.* But I feel like it's for the greater benefit."

———

Nick and Muriel talk through everything in their relationship, but they haven't been able to discuss whether to have biological children as openly as they have other dilemmas. "For the longest time, it felt like something we could decide later, and that's coming to an end, so frankly we're not very good at this new conversation," Nick says.

Muriel agrees with Nick that this feels like the one aspect of their life they might be aging out of. "I'm not tripping about what type of adult I need to be by a certain age," she says, "but with the kid stuff, it's like the beating of the Telltale Heart. Eventually I can't think my way out of it, or justify it. It will just end up happening that I'm not able to have kids biologically anymore."

She keeps thinking about it, and has lots of friends having children now, but "the main difference is they really wanted to and they figured out a way," she says. "They're excited and happy. I think I would just be stressed." Committing to trying to get pregnant, now or in a year or so, feels like she'd be going into a fight she doesn't want to be in. "It all seems like joining a battlefield, going into survival mode, and trying to protect your eggs," she says. "And then I can't even think about what it would be like to have a baby. It just feels like a grenade."

That she can't visualize having biological children makes her most sure she doesn't want to do it. "I can kind of picture doing better in my life and looking at adoption and fostering, but I just have a blank spot for what being pregnant and giving birth to a child would look like. I'm like, *Where would that fit in?*"

Nick, too, can't see how they could take care of a child right now, when "we don't have a solid foundation to build on," he says. "I don't mean monetarily. We don't know where we're going to be in a year. There's so much that we're unsure of."

Some friends have encouraged Muriel to just try to get pregnant, to see what happens, but "that seems like a really bad idea," she says. "I don't want to take that risk. I do worry that I'm missing out on something. I'm human and I don't want to miss out on the fundamental human thing. But my only conflict is that. I don't have a conflict of, *Oh, I wish I was sitting here with a baby on my lap.*"

———

I did not get pregnant immediately. I went through a year of fertility treatments, and a miscarriage, before I ended up where I am as I write this: seven months into a pregnancy that has been successful so far.

I am lucky to have had both the money and health insurance for these treatments, and to have had my body respond to them. There were times when I was trying to get pregnant that I didn't think I would be able to. I am wary of causing pain to anyone who is struggling with their own fertility, but during those periods of uncertainty, I tried hard to stay open. I might not have biological children, but there were options beyond that, including using a donor egg, adopting, or not having children. That wasn't what I was trying to do, aggressively and expensively, at the moment, and I know I would have felt crushed if I were told that it was pointless to keep using my own eggs.

But I also know that during this time I felt different than I did in my early thirties, when I had this set path and any deviation from it was terrifying, like taking even a small step sideways would decimate who I thought I was going to be. Now I understood that no matter what my life looked like, I knew who I was. If it was too late for me to get pregnant, that would have to be okay. I hadn't been ready before.

What I hope for in having a child isn't any sort of completion. I'm scared in a way that maybe I shouldn't admit that being a mom *is* some sort of an end, and that it will make me stop pushing on all the parts of my life that I already love.

I went for a walk with Ruthie the other day in the park by our apartments at a period in my pregnancy when I was acutely nervous about the shake-up this baby would cause. She doesn't have kids, and I am worried that me having a baby might weaken our friendship. This fear came out sloppily in the midst of a conversation about a completely different topic, when I said abruptly, "I don't want things to change."

"I don't want them to either," she replied instantly, as if she'd been waiting to blurt the same thing.

In the same way, when my boyfriend and I were getting ready to go to sleep one night, I rushed over to his side of the bed to confess I was nervous about the baby taking away from our relationship. "I like how this is," I said, "but there will be another person here soon, and I'm afraid we'll no longer be us."

He kissed me, which is what he usually does to show me that he gets what I'm saying while he works out how he wants to respond. After a moment, he said, "I think we will be."

I don't know what will happen, but what I hope is that having a child becomes another part of my life that I love, not that it makes me any more adult. In sociologists' eyes this may be another step that turns me into one, but I am already there. I'm not looking for an anchor. I'm looking for an entirely new experience. I wasn't sure I wanted this experience for a long time, and even after I was, I wasn't sure how to make it happen, but I've arrived at it now.

CONCLUSION

———

It's awesome to watch your dreams grow and yourself get better at being a person and navigating the world, but the other part is the world seems like it's falling apart.

—MURIEL

In Austin, after the night he found himself crying on his couch, Marcus finally made an appointment with a therapist. He hoped she could help him stop feeling so bad about not being able to make what he wants happen. He's had a few sessions, but isn't sure therapy is working. He doesn't feel different, and the therapist won't give him anything that he can use as a guide to evaluate if he's improving, "things I can work on," he says. Right now, "I just go and talk to her." He doesn't mind this but wishes it were more clear the practice was doing something.

He also got offered a new job, but it's within the same company. The only thing he'd be changing is getting away from his current department. Marcus wasn't excited. "Oh man, it's a lateral move," he told L.

She pointed out that even so, at least he'd be leaving the job he had to fight to get out of bed to go to. She wanted him to be at least a little happy. *Would you take five minutes to be excited?* she said.

"I logically recognize I should be more excited," he says. "But it's still with the same company. Some of it's going to be more of the same. It's not a dream job. It's just another job."

His therapist pointed out that he has a tendency to dismiss anything positive he's done and, instead, see only failure and what he needs to work toward next. "You don't recognize your accomplishments, or you underplay them," she told him.

To one session, he showed up with a list of what happened that week: what pissed him off, what pissed him off that he resolved, and what pissed him off that wasn't that bad.

His therapist listened, then said, "Did anything good happen?"

"It gave me perspective," Marcus says. "Three bad things happened, but four good things happened, and some of them were bigger than the bad things."

A good thing that happened is that Marcus's new job means that he'll be staying in Austin. L can finally plan her move. Marcus is going to fly to Chicago and help her pack, whenever she's ready. "I just need a date," he says.

———

Over Labor Day weekend, Marcus flew to Chicago to help L move. They packed her apartment but put most of her belongings in storage for professional movers to take later, and she and Marcus flew back to Austin with four bags. "It all went perfect," he says.

L hadn't wanted to live with him if they weren't engaged, but her company, that she was now working for remotely, was threatening layoffs. She might lose her income, so she moved into Marcus's apartment.

He's happy she's there. The bathroom is too small for both of them (he wishes they had two sinks) and they stack clean dishes differently (they could use a bigger counter). But unlike with previous girlfriends, with L, he's never tried to fake like he's perfect, which makes it easier to live together. "I used to try to be this man that I think this woman wants," he says. "That blew up in my face, so then I was like, Let me try being myself. In my head, I was like, *Ain't nobody going to like that*, but someone did."

He's already bored at his new job. His boss gave him a month to do a project, and Marcus completed it in two weeks. "I'm done with that thing," he told his boss.

"Nah, hold it," his boss said. "I don't want to rush anybody. Why don't you review your notes?"

What was I thinking getting this done early? Marcus fumed as he walked back to his desk with two weeks to sit around.

"That core problem is still there," he says. "I'm doing something that is not fulfilling. I feel like that's a very millennial thing to want to derive purpose from work. I find that annoying about myself. It sounds corny. But that is fundamentally what's bothering me. Whether I went to work or not, would it matter?"

After getting no job offers for more than two years, Marcus got an offer from another company just four weeks after he started his new job. It's still an auditing job, but it's working with community housing and development in Houston, to provide people with low and moderate incomes places to live. When he went to the interview, there were people walking in from off the street saying, *Hey, I need help. Who do I talk to?* Marcus could actually see who'd be affected by his work, unlike with his current work for the state, where "I crunch these numbers, I do these audits, and it feels like, *So what?*" he says. "That's a year of my time but what did this audit do? It's hard to connect what you did for forty hours a week to an outcome."

He wanted to take the job and move to Houston, but L also had a new job opportunity, and hers was in Austin. Marcus argued that he'd asked for a $10,000 raise from this new company, money that he planned to put into his financial-advice business. He hasn't given up on wanting to make teaching and speaking gigs his only job. This was a way of having some money to promote the business and see if enough people hired him. "I'd like to see what happens," he says.

But L didn't think they should automatically take Marcus's job offer. They were happy in Austin, and what if her job opportunity also came with a raise? She was willing to let Marcus use her extra money for his business too. "I've never had anybody remotely close to saying, 'I'll support you in this endeavor that might blow up in your face,'" Marcus says. "'You can use the raise. You're not in this alone.'"

———

In the spring of 2020, the coronavirus pandemic sent us all into our homes and centered our lives around safety and shelter. Even if we were lucky enough not to have anyone close to us die or get sick, or get sick ourselves, our lives changed and continue to change. What might have seemed in reach before might now seem like it's out of the frame completely. Or we may no longer want what we once did.

To me, what's happening seems like a doubling down on what I suspected when I was first looking back on my own thirties and how they didn't line up in the orderly way I thought they would: We're never finished. As we continue to define our adulthoods, this message might as well be scrawled in neon across our days.

In theory, we have freedom to do what we want, when we want. We can do work that provides us with more than just a paycheck. We can marry or not. We can buy a home, or we can decide we'd rather not live anywhere too long. We can have kids or choose not to.

But, in part, it can feel like we're declining or delaying these things because we can't actually achieve them. There is a sense that even if we felt like replicating what's seen as a traditional adulthood we wouldn't be able to. We couldn't get to the milestones that were so easy to get to in the past. They're no longer in reach for us. How can we afford to buy a home? How can we be sure we should marry this person? Is job security even possible? How can we raise a child if we want one?

"It's easy to think, *Something's wrong. Either with me, or my generation, or my potential mate, since we can't make those markers anymore*," says Stephanie Coontz.

Constructing these raised-stakes adulthoods takes longer, and in some cases, to be brutally honest, may not happen. We may have too much debt. We may not find the right relationship at the right time. We may not be able to make it in our ideal career. We may make mistakes we can't undo. We may not be able to afford our dreams. People who have the same aspirations and talents aren't necessarily going to end up with the same successes. It's not true that if you don't get something you desire, you should have tried harder. Everyone does not have the same opportunities, even if we should. We're all pushed forward, and held back, by our backgrounds, our financial cushions or lack thereof, and our personalities, as well as luck and so many other tangible and in-tangible factors. And as COVID-19 laid bare, things in life can suddenly be out of our control.

"There are people who can't make the lives they want," Coontz says. "And that's scary."

———

Charles is taking the second-to-last class that he needs to finish before he graduates and is getting an A, a grade he's motivated to go after because he wants to earn a high enough GPA to get accepted to a good MBA program. Hopefully, having an MBA will help him become a partner at the construction firm someday. He's trying to stop telling himself that life will be better when he finishes school, in part because he wants to continue on for his MBA, but also because "I have to stop saying, *I'll be happy when this is done*," he says. "There's always going to be that next thing, especially if I'm going to try to keep doing better."

He and Matt talked more about marriage, and Matt asked how Charles would feel if he was never ready. At first Charles said he'd want to break up, which upset Matt. Usually they would have had a fight and taken some space from each other for a few days. But because of the lockdown they were stuck in the house together, so they kept talking. Charles ended up confessing that he's afraid Matt doesn't want to get married because he's waiting for someone better.

"I told myself that he wasn't saying yes because of any number of insecurities," he says. "I haven't finished my degree yet, he likes someone else, my credit score is worse than his, and on and on."

Matt told Charles that wasn't true, that his hesitation is about himself, and that he's still working on himself and his own issues.

"I rarely talk about my insecurities with him, because I am afraid of how crazy he will think I am," Charles says. "It was nice to hear he feels the same way, just like every other human on earth."

———

Marcus got offered the job, and the raise he wanted, in Houston, while L didn't get the job she was interviewing for in Austin, so they decided to move to Houston. Marcus had his final day at his old job on a Friday, they moved over the weekend, and he started the new job on Monday. They signed an eighteen-month lease for "the nicest apartment I've ever been in in my life," he says. "It's growing on me."

His life is morphing, but not necessarily in the way he had anticipated. He still works as an auditor, and even though his new job is a promotion, he wears a suit and tie to the office and "at the end of the day, it's work," he says. He's continuing to build his financial-education business, but for the moment, he's accepted that "maybe I am an auditor," he says. "I'm good at it."

He wasn't looking for a serious relationship either, but he's in one and likes it. L wanted to be engaged before they lived together, and even though that didn't happen, she still wanted to get engaged. Marcus promised her he'd propose, and "I want to stick to my promise," he says. "I do love her. I think I'm personally agnostic about marriage, as a means to an end, but I logically recognize the comfort, security, and guarantee it brings."

He planned to propose on his birthday or New Year's Eve, but when he asked L her ring size, she told him she wanted to pick out her own ring. So he's waiting for her to do that, and then he'll pick another date. "I don't know when I'm going to propose yet," he says, "but I look forward to it."

Marcus isn't entirely comfortable with all these changes. In some ways he still feels as out of control as he did before he found another job and L moved. How should this new future go? He wants to plan it out, too. What are his priorities? Marriage? His financial-education business? Kids? Making more money?

His therapist warned against him continuing to micromanage his life. Before he left for Houston, they had a final session.

It's okay to be anxious, she told him. *It's okay to not know what's coming next.*

Marcus is trying to follow her guidance and to dial back his need to dictate how everything will go. "It clearly wears me down, this inability to turn off," he says. "I'm trying to be okay not knowing what's going to happen."

Instead, he's going to try to construct his life using the same philosophy he did with LEGO sets as a kid. Back then he'd put the blocks together as best as he could and not care if what he built looked like the picture on the box. After all, no one but him knew what it was supposed to turn out like. It's the same with his life. "I'm trying to make it mine," he says. "Hopefully it comes out pretty on the other end, but even if it doesn't, I have the box. I'm the only one who knows what it should look like."

———

Nick got another bartending job before his unemployment ran out, so he'd be making money while he kept looking for assistant jobs, but restaurants in LA were closed a few weeks later due to the pandemic. He and Muriel have been working when they can, with Muriel doing takeout orders at her restaurant and Nick waiting tables on the patio at his, but they are largely unemployed. Their comedy work is mostly nonexistent too: the clubs where Nick did stand-up are closed, as is Muriel's improv theater, and there are no more in-person auditions for commercials.

When everything they once did in LA stopped or slowed, Nick felt a huge amount of relief, which he was surprised by. He knew he'd been feeling badly about himself, how he was trying to get an assistant job and couldn't. He'd been waking up in the middle of night, certain that he'd done his whole life wrong. "I was constantly feeling like I was in last place, that I was this horrific failure," he says. "I couldn't keep up with the crowd."

But he was still going to auditions and stand-up shows and interviews when he could get them, and thought he would continue to. Then the shutdown happened. "When they pulled the plug on the world, suddenly I could breathe," he says. "I couldn't keep up with the crowd, and then, now, it's like there is no more crowd."

They know that the pause is just that, and that even if what they built their life out of in LA doesn't return, eventually they'll have to figure out how to make money—their savings, what they make from their podcast, and unemployment money will last about another six months. But for now, they bought fancy lawn chairs and took them up to the roof of their building, where they lay in the sun. They've also been fostering kittens, who were terrified of Nick and Muriel at first but then slowly got used to them and want to sleep on their necks, which Muriel loves. They marched in Black Lives Matter protests, and at the first one, Muriel started sobbing behind her face mask, remembering her dad being pulled over when she was a teenager. The police officer didn't believe Muriel was his daughter because she looks white. Instead, he accused her of being a prostitute.

"I was just like crying the entire time," she says. "I guess I have some trauma that I haven't processed. My brain was like, *I did not expect that to happen.*"

She and Nick have long talks about what they might want to

change in their life, usually at night when they take two-hour walks. Muriel is savoring the chance to think about what she was doing every day. She wonders if she was getting caught up in auditioning for commercials, which she didn't really like, or taking extra shifts at the restaurant to pay for the increasing cost of their health insurance, because that was what she thought she should be doing, not because it was making her happy. What would she do if she were less wrapped up in her ambition? The future feels far enough away that it's fun to speculate about. Maybe they'll move to Utah, where Nick's brother is. Or they could buy a camper, or go back to school, or open their own little restaurant.

"Anything you can think of, it's on the table," Muriel says. "It's just this funny thing of when everything gets stripped away you start thinking about fundamental things. It's been weird to feel like, *I want to burn everything to the ground.*"

———

In September, both of Adam's daughters were supposed to be in school, giving him an empty house during the day for the first time since he became a dad, but right now, he's not sure if school is going to start in the fall. Instead, all Adam can visualize is the rest of the summer—the girls playing in an inflatable pool in the backyard, him doling out snacks every five minutes while trying to keep working on his book. He's channeling his anxiety into his writing instead of questions about the next few months, or even the next year. When he's thinking positively he can see some kind of normal on the other end of this time, "but I don't know when we'll get to that," he says. "I can't wrap my brain around that. I can see something on the other end of this, but I find it very hard to think about the process of getting there."

———

We are going to get old. It's inevitable.

When I was crying to my mom, who's in her late seventies, about my failed proposal, I wailed, "I'm so old."

She said, "You're not old, sweetheart. *I'm* old."

I don't think of her that way. Last year we went to Rome, and she marched me around on four-hour tours of ruins every day while maintaining the same energy she had at hour one until hour four.

Tom W. Smith, the former director of the General Social Survey, points out that an often forgotten occurrence happening alongside adulthood being approached at a later age is that we're also living longer than we used to. In 2018, life expectancy at birth rose to 78.7 years, according to the National Center for Health Statistics.

"There is this delay of the full implementation of adulthood at the beginning of the life cycle, but there is also an extension at the end," Smith says. "The proportion of the population living to eighty or ninety is continuing to go up, so adulthood is shrinking at the younger ages but extending at the older ages. It's a way I don't hear expressed very often, but if you didn't start adulthood until you were in your thirties, you would still have as many years of adulthood now as you would have in the 1950s or 1960s. It's not just a delay, but it's a shift too. The delay is the more important part of the story, but it's also an upward shift in the life cycle."

But regardless of when we feel old, or use the label, the truth is there is a point when you will feel as though you've learned more than you have yet to learn, that you no longer have as much emptiness and choice in front of you as you once did. The space between the chaos and the shape of your life lessens.

———

Yasin moved from Jersey City to Raleigh, North Carolina. Now that no one was having business meetings in person, he no longer felt like he needed to be near New York. He and Melanie debated where they wanted to live, considering Atlanta and Austin along with Raleigh, before renting a three-bedroom apartment in Raleigh through a video tour. For the drive, his brother who he'd talked with through the night in Kuala Lumpur accompanied Yasin in the moving truck while Melanie and Leyla followed in their new car. When Yasin locked the door of his Jersey City apartment for the last time, he felt the finality of the moment. He thought, *This is really happening.* But he wasn't sad to leave.

"It was more like the rush when you're climbing on a roller coaster and you know there's a big drop coming," he says. "There was anticipation and excitement." They drove for the next twelve hours. As they did, Yasin and his brother talked about their dad.

Yasin's brother speculated about how proud he must be of them. Yasin thinks this is true, that it must be nice for his dad to look back on coming to the United States with nothing and know that his sons are making their own lives and doing well. Someday, he hopes he can feel the same way about Leyla.

When they got to Raleigh around 1:00 a.m., Yasin was giddy partly because he was exhausted from the drive, but also because they were finally there. Even though it was dark, he could see how much more space there was, both outside and in their new apartment. "It was like, *It's real*," he says. "This is our new home."

———

Abigail's eighty-five-year-old grandmother, who had been rooting for Abigail to give her a great-grandbaby, has been ill, and her memory has been foggy. But, in September, they had a conversation where she was like her old self, enthusiastically asking Abigail about "your plan," an allusion to when she was going to have a baby on her own. Abigail told her that she thought she'd be pregnant by now. Her grandmother replied, "Well, what are you waiting for?"

"The conversation just hit me differently than it had before," Abigail says. She realized she wasn't waiting for anything.

She's a lot happier in her new real estate career. "I'm helping people," she says. "I'm helping them move on to the next chapter. Every client at the closing table says the kindest things."

And she's no longer torn about needing to find a romantic

partner before having a child. Her desire to be a mother far out-weighs her desire to be a wife or a girlfriend. Her friends all knew she was thinking about becoming a solo parent, too. "It was clear that there was literally nothing holding me back," she says. She was ready to try to have a child on her own.

Abigail began searching for a sperm donor and eventually chose one who is tall with dark hair, like her, and got a 1540 on his SATs. Around the same time she settled on a donor, however, her grandmother was hospitalized with COVID-19, which she probably won't survive.

Even so, Abigail is going ahead with her plan. She's scheduled for an intrauterine injection (doctors advised that she save her frozen eggs until she's older). "The fact that I am now trying to get pregnant as my grandmother is in her final days has been dif-ficult to process, but it hasn't given me any doubts," she says. "Life's timing never really makes any sense."

———

"There's a sense that you can't do everything in life," says Kieran Setiya, a professor of philosophy at the Massachusetts Institute of Technology and the author of *Midlife: A Philosophical Guide*, "that your choices are going to close out options, or the sense that there are regrets in your past, things you wish you hadn't done or you wished hadn't happened to you. You can change where in life and how early in your life you're forced to confront those issues, but I think almost anyone who's reflective about their life is at some

point going to feel the need to come to terms with the limited-
ness of what it's possible for them to do in their life."

What's missing in seeing this as complete loss, though, is the
beauty in getting to this point. That tightening you feel when
choices get taken away is a reflection of something good: that you
had the choices to begin with. We are lucky that our lives haven't
been decided for us, that we weren't centered over one ideal and
told that's all there is and will ever be.

"Imagine what it would be like not to be faced with those
kinds of painful decisions," Setiya says. "The only way to avoid
them is you'd have to be monomaniacal. You'd have to be someone for whom there was only one thing you valued at all, and
that's a very impoverished life to have. To some degree, just
thinking through the inevitability of regret, if you're open to
enough different kinds of things and capable of appreciating
them, well that's wonderful, and if you are, you're going to be
faced with choices in which something is lost."

That you have to make choices, that you aren't able to do everything, isn't a sign of a life gone wrong. The fact that you're
open to various routes, to going sideways or upside down or back-
ward, means it has gone right: you found meaning and value in
many different ways of living. To be able to have that in our thirties at this moment in time is a privilege, one that those who
came before us didn't always have. It's something to embrace
rather than recoil from.

———

Sally is single again. She and Jay had their first humongous fight, where she left the apartment, then he left, and, even after both of them came back, they didn't speak to each other for the rest of the night. In the morning, they started talking and spent the next few days discussing their relationship, a conversation Jay mostly led. He told Sally he wasn't happy; he hated how her opinions always dominated his.

"You never let me talk," he yelled during their fight. "You always think that you're right." But more important, he was questioning his sexuality and realizing more and more that he might be attracted to women *and* men. This was and wasn't a surprise to Sally.

"There are so many guys that I date when I start dating them, I'm like, *I don't know if you're as straight as you think you are.* Jay was that way too, where I wondered, but then I was like, *Okay, you're straight, okay, sure.* I'm not going to question somebody's sexuality."

She's preparing to move into her own apartment, the first time she's ever lived by herself, and is excited to be in charge of her own space and time. "I'm going to be responsible for how I live every day," she says. "I don't have to check with anyone about what I'm doing."

She's looking for two-bedroom places, so she can have an office and no longer have to work on the dining room table or in bed. She also wants a lot of kitchen-counter space, so she can get back to baking, and "I've become obsessed with having a pink sofa," she says.

Part of her is mourning the end of the relationship and what it means for her life, but the other part is optimistic that the future will be better. "There's that worry that this was it," she says. "This was my chance, and now I'm going to be alone forever, but I don't know that's the case. I think I'm such a different person now than I was when the relationship started, and this was a wonderful thing that happened. I'm still really hopeful about what the hell life is going to bring."

————

On New Year's Day this year, my boyfriend, Ruthie, and another friend named Oakley decided to drive to the beach and dive in the ocean. We'd come up with the plan the night before at Ruthie's, when she had people over for dinner. I've spent a lot of New Year's Eves at Ruthie's, and many of them have been when I was at what felt like turning points in my life. One year, before going over to her house, I'd spent the day moving out of the apartment I rented with a roommate to the one my parents helped me buy, where I was going to live alone. Another, I had just returned to New York, numb and stumbling after my failed proposal. This year, I was pregnant.

I usually make large-scale New Year's resolutions, not about ways I want to live more healthily or thoughtfully, but about life goals I want to accomplish, like "get engaged" or "finish book."

I hadn't written anything down by the time I went to Ruthie's that night. I told myself I'd have to do it the next day. As the evening went on, at one point, well after midnight, Ruthie said, "I have an idea. Do you want to drive to the beach tomorrow and put our feet in the water?"

My boyfriend countered, "If we're doing that, we're going all the way in."

So on New Year's Day, at 2:00 p.m., we forced ourselves off our respective couches and into the car. As we drove to Coney Island, it was about forty degrees and windy. I love Coney Island. The wooden Cyclone, with its steep drops and no loops, is my all-time favorite roller coaster, and seeing it behind us as we walked to the beach made me feel calm.

We stripped to our bathing suits and raced to the water. There was no point in overthinking how cold it would be. I was last and watched my friends submerge themselves into the ocean, leaving splashes where they once stood. But even though I was waist-deep in ice water, I couldn't make myself dive. *Keep going*, I commanded myself, and finally went under too. My friends sprinted out of the water, and I tried to run after them, but my legs were tingling, my top half was too heavy, and I couldn't pick up my feet. By the time I made it near the shore, they were running to me, holding out their hands and towels.

As we wrapped ourselves in all the warm clothing we'd brought and took triumphant pictures on the beach, the sun was setting. The fading light formed a halo around the boardwalk and the water. I thought about it being a new year and a new decade, in time and in my life. But I didn't think about how I hadn't written any goals or how, specifically, my life wasn't laid out like I wanted it to be. I didn't think about how I wasn't married or that

I was about to be living in a one-bedroom apartment with a baby. I thought only about how glad I was to be on the beach—the sand, the water, and the people I love were sparkling—and about taking these experiences as I get them. I thought only about getting back in the car and continuing on.

Keep going, I thought.

I did not know that in a few months I'd be finishing this book at the kitchen table with my four-month-old son next to me, while my boyfriend worked from home in the bedroom instead of at the office he used to go to every day. In a practical sense, none of us have anywhere to go, but in an abstract one, this setup seems like the ultimate proof that even as I soul-searched and fumbled to structure my life pretty closely to the one I'm living now, I still have to keep going. The everyday choices I had thought were settled no longer are: How will we build a new community for the moment? What will I do for work? What kind of world will my son grow up in? What was I doing out of habit that I no longer want to do? The more change that happens, the more I understand that no one decision will make my life, and this is not the end either.

Someday, of course, there will be a flatness, a plateau where we know we've made most of our choices. When we get there we may be scraped or bruised. We may be exhilarated. We may be wondering, *Is this it?* But no matter what, the spot we stop at will be ours alone, where we've arrived because of what we went after, what we decided we didn't want, and what we had to let go. And in all likelihood, we will be somewhere we couldn't see until we were standing there because, before then, we were still so young.

SELECTED BIBLIOGRAPHY

INTRODUCTION

Arnett, Jeffrey Jensen. "Emerging Adulthood." *American Psychologist* 55, no. 5 (May 2000): 469–80.

Furstenberg, Frank F., Jr., Sheela Kennedy, Vonnie C. McLoyd, Rubén G. Rumbaut, and Richard A. Settersten Jr. "Growing Up Is Harder to Do." *Contexts* 3, no. 3 (August 2004): 33–41.

CHAPTER ONE: COMPLETING SCHOOL

Collins, Randall. *The Credential Society: An Historical Sociology of Education and Stratification.* New York: Columbia University Press, 2019.

Coontz, Stephanie. *The Way We Never Were: American Families and the Nostalgia Trap.* Revised and updated ed. New York: Basic Books, 2016.

Herbold, Hilary. "Never a Level Playing Field: Blacks and the GI Bill." *The Journal of Blacks in Higher Education,* no. 6 (Winter 1994–1995): 104–08.

Katznelson, Ira. *When Affirmative Action Was White: An Untold History of Racial Inequality in Twentieth-Century America.* New York: W. W. Norton, 2006.

Miller, M. H. "Been Down So Long It Looks Like Debt to Me." *Baffler,* no. 40 (July 2018).

Mintz, Steven. *The Prime of Life: A History of Modern Adulthood.* Cambridge, MA: Belknap Press of Harvard University Press, 2015.

Tough, Paul. *The Years That Matter Most: How College Makes or Breaks Us.* Boston: Houghton Mifflin Harcourt, 2019.

BIBLIOGRAPHY

CHAPTER TWO: LEAVING HOME

Aarons, Leroy F. "'Don't Trust Anybody Over 30': Phrasemaker, at 30, Still Radical." *Washington Post*, March 23, 1970.

Brown, Kelly Williams. *Adulting: How to Become a Grown-Up in 468 Easy(ish) Steps*. New York: Grand Central, 2013.

Huber, Lucy. "My Husband and I Couldn't Get Jobs, So We Moved into My Parents' Retirement Community." *HuffPost*, September, 18, 2018, https://www.huffpost.com/entry/moving-into-a-retirement-community_n_5b466a92e4b0e7c958f770ed.

Keniston, Kenneth. "Youth: A 'New' Stage of Life." *American Scholar* 39, no. 4 (Autumn 1970): 631–54.

Pinsker, Joe. "The New Boomerang Kids Could Change American Views of Living at Home." *Atlantic*, July 3, 2020, https://www.theatlantic.com/family/archive/2020/07/pandemic-young-adults-living-with-parents/613723/.

Sheehy, Gail. *Passages: Predictable Crises of Adult Life*. New York: Dutton, 2013.

Steinberg, Laurence. "The Case for Delayed Adulthood." *New York Times*, September 19, 2014, https://www.nytimes.com/2014/09/21/opinion/sunday/the-case-for-delayed-adulthood.html.

CHAPTER THREE: MARRYING

Filipovic, Jill. *The H-Spot: The Feminist Pursuit of Happiness*. New York: Bold Type Books, 2018.

Jay, Meg. *The Defining Decade: Why Your Twenties Matter—and How to Make the Most of Them*. New York: Twelve, 2013.

Traister, Rebecca. *All the Single Ladies: Unmarried Women and the Rise of an Independent Nation*. New York: Simon & Schuster, 2016.

CHAPTER FOUR: BECOMING FINANCIALLY INDEPENDENT

Collins, Chuck. *Born on Third Base: A One Percenter Makes the Case for Tackling Inequality, Bringing Wealth Home, and Committing to the Common Good*. White River Junction, VT: Chelsea Green, 2016.

Cramer, Reid. *The Emerging Millennial Wealth Gap*. Washington, DC: New America, 2019.

Hacker, Jacob S., and Paul Pierson. *American Amnesia: How the War on Government Led Us to Forget What Made America Prosper.* New York: Simon & Schuster, 2017.

Kreizman, Maris. "Where Did My Ambition Go?" Medium, June 26, 2020, https://gen.medium.com/where-did-my-ambition-go-c800ab4ad01d.

Petersen, Anne Helen. "How Millennials Became The Burnout Generation." BuzzFeed *News*, January 5, 2019, https://www.buzzfeednews.com/article/annehelenpetersen/millennials-burnout-generation-debt-work.

Porter, Eduardo, and David Yaffe-Bellany. "Facing Adulthood with an Economic Disaster's Lasting Scars." *New York Times*, May 19, 2020, https://www.nytimes.com/2020/05/19/business/economy/coronavirus-young-old.html.

Seligson, Hannah. "The New 30-Something." *New York Times*, March 2, 2019, https://www.nytimes.com/2019/03/02/style/financial-independence-30s.html.

Wang, Connie. "The 'Grateful to Be Here' Generation Has Some Apologizing to Do." Refinery29, June 22, 2020, https://www.refinery29.com/en-us/2020/06/9867469/working-in-toxic-media-industry-diversity-movement.

CHAPTER FIVE: HAVING A CHILD

Adamy, Janet. "U.S. Birthrates Fall to Record Low. *Wall Street Journal*, May 20, 2020, https://www.wsj.com/articles/u-s-birthrates-fall-to-record-low-11589947260.

Miller, Claire Cain. "The 10-Year Baby Window That Is the Key to the Women's Pay Gap." *New York Times*, April 9, 2018, https://www.nytimes.com/2018/04/09/upshot/the-10-year-baby-window-that-is-the-key-to-the-womens-pay-gap.html.

Yuhas, Alan. "Don't Expect a Quarantine Baby Boom." *New York Times*, April 8, 2020, https://www.nytimes.com/2020/04/08/us/coronavirus-baby-boom.html.

CONCLUSION

Setiya, Kieran. *Midlife: A Philosophical Guide.* Princeton, NJ: Princeton University Press, 2018.

ACKNOWLEDGMENTS

Endless thanks to Marcus, Charles, Yasin, Sally, Nick, Muriel, Adam, and Abigail, who said yes to letting a stranger write about their lives. They are the heart of this book.

I'm hugely inspired by and indebted to Maya Ziv, who pushed me to make this book bigger and better, then to rethink and rewrite it when the world changed.

Thank you to everyone at Dutton for believing in me and being willing to do this a second time, especially Emily Canders; I'm forever grateful to Allison Hunter for insisting this idea was the right one.

Andrea Woo is my first reader. Not having her guidance would be like losing a limb.

When I was struggling with how to distill a decade, Mamie Healey suggested I tell the stories of real thirtysomethings, and that made all the difference. Carrie Frye told me to just start swimming, and thanks to her, I did.

Aileen Boyle understood the book immediately—and, more important, who needed to read it.

ACKNOWLEDGMENTS

Thanks on repeat to the readers, librarians, and booksellers who supported *Text Me When You Get Home.*

So much love to my friends whom I trust with my life and who trust me with theirs: Matthew Collins-Gibson, Valerie Johnson, Stephanie Clifford, Erica Cerulo, Claire Mazur, Marisa Meltzer, Amanda Dobbins, Yaran Noti, Julia Chang, Jaison Joseph, Oakley Olson, Kim Warner, Nien Lam, Andrea Oliveri, Nicole Vecchiarelli, Carmel Melouney, Albert Chen, and Thomas Hauner.

I'm so glad my mom is my mom, and that she pushes me to be more optimistic, which she's right about more often than not; thank you to my dad and brother, who are in my head and heart.

Ruthie Baron held my hand through my thirties and is the absolute best. I constantly think about how cool she is and marvel that I get to be her friend.

Julien du Castel delights me every day, and I'm grateful to him for opening his arms to me again and again. Thank you for making me so happy.

And finally, I'm continually charmed by Vincent du Castel, whose life is just beginning, but whose smile is already legendary.

ABOUT THE AUTHOR

Kayleen Schaefer is a journalist and author of *Text Me When You Get Home* and the bestselling Kindle Single memoir *Fade Out*. Her work has appeared in the *New York Times*, *Vanity Fair*, the *New Yorker*, *Vogue*, and many other publications. She lives in New York City.